THE PATH

Ten Simple Steps to a Guaranteed Life of Happiness

WILLIAM R. ENGLISH

ISBN 978-1-63575-120-8 (Paperback)
ISBN 978-1-63575-121-5 (Digital)

Christian Faith Publishing, Inc.
296 Chestnut Street
Meadville, PA 16335
www.christianfaithpublishing.com

Printed in the United States of America

DEDICATION

To my dad, my role model, who, by example,
has taught me the value of hard work.

To my wife, my miracle. You are proof that God's love endures.

And to my Heavenly Father. Despite being lost, I
am now found. You never abandoned me. Without
You, this book would not be possible.

Contents

Welcome

Let me begin by saying welcome and congratulations on the beginning of your journey. Something important that I would like you to know is that I do not think it is a coincidence that you are reading this right now. As a matter of fact, I believe that you are reading this book because you are looking for something more out of life. Call it destiny if you will, but I think that you are reading this book right now because you are ready for a change. And not just a small change, but a big change, a drastic change, a change of momentous proportions, and it begins right now. I believe that by the time you finish reading this book, you will have experienced the dramatic change that you've been searching for. It will not only be a change in your life but also in you how you view the world. It will be a change for the better, and when you are done, you will never be the same. I believe that you will create a life even greater than you have ever dreamed of or imagined! So get excited and be prepared because you are about to embark on a journey that will ultimately become the beginning of your new life!

What Exactly Is Happiness?

Before we commence, I feel as though it is important to take a minute and discuss what exactly it means to be happy. According to *Merriam-Webster*'s online dictionary, *happiness* is defined as "a state of well-being and contentment." Although the minutiae details of what a happy life would entail may vary from person to person, the purpose of this book is to provide a guide so that every individual can enjoy a happy life. The happiness that I am referring to is a life-long feeling of positivity, contentment, joy, gratitude, and fulfillment where one can feel at peace.

It is important not to confuse happiness with experiencing pleasure. Although pleasure can be attained and experienced while being happy, the goal of this book is not temporary pleasure, but rather a life full of happiness and fulfillment.

Before going any further, it would be remiss of me if I did not mention one important fact. The one thing that is imperative for you to know and understand before going any further on this journey is that *you* are in full control of your own level of happiness and ultimately the quality of your life! It is not your mother or father, husband or wife, not even the president of the United States that will determine whether or not you will be happy for the rest of your life on earth, but rather you and you alone.

One final but essential fact that I want you to know is that I firmly believe that life is meant to be enjoyed. I also believe that our Father in heaven wants nothing more than for us to be happy. He has given each of us the power to determine for ourselves whether or not we will be happy in this life, but ultimately He leaves it up to us to decide.

I wholeheartedly believe that the steps laid out before you in this book can and will allow you to live the life that you've always desired, but only if you choose to put forth the effort and apply the knowledge laid out before you. With that being said, read on and best of luck. Happiness awaits!

Why Write This book?

I felt that it would only be fair to include a minibiography of my life in order to give you some perspective and enlighten you a bit as to where I have been and where I am coming from in writing this book. The purpose of this book is to offer insight and direct you to the path that I believe will allow you to find direction and create a life that you know is possible yet can't seem to find.

After all, despite some of the details being different, many of us experience the same types of ups and downs in life, as well as the emotions that go along with them.

Let me begin by saying that a number of years ago, I found myself in a very dark place. At that time, I felt extremely lost and uncertain as to where my life was heading. My despair must have been evident to those around me because on a number of occasions, individuals with whom I was the closest inquired as to whether or not I was okay. Like most people who are struggling in life, I told them that I was fine and did my best to put on a facade of happiness, but on the inside, I was hurting and desperate.

I didn't like my life, and I didn't like the person that I had become. I knew that things could get better. I knew that this wasn't the life that God had intended for me. I also knew that it was only a matter of finding the right direction in order to get my life on track. I desperately wanted to find the correct method of living.

I knew that there was a particular *way* of living that would be pleasing to God, but I wasn't quite sure as to how to find it. I knew that I needed Christ in my life. As a matter of fact, early followers of Christ were not referred to as Christians, but rather followers of "the Way," for they were followers of the Way that Christ had taught them to live through His words and by His example, as well as the Way that their Heavenly Father wanted them to live (Acts 9:2, NIV).

Although I knew this in my heart, it would take years of trial and error (a lot of error) for me to discover what it would take to find and maintain true happiness in life.

When writing this book, I came to the realization that many people may ask the question as to why a history teacher from a small town in Pennsylvania would feel qualified or even inclined to offer insights on how to attain lifelong happiness and fulfillment. I believe this to be a completely fair question, and if I were in the reader's shoes, I believe that I too would be asking the very same thing. Therefore, I will do my best to keep this explanation short and to the point but also attempt to be as thorough as possible in my explanation as to why I felt compelled to write this book.

A Little about My Life...and Maybe Yours

I believe that in order to gain a better understanding of my perspective on happiness, it is important to understand how it is that I've arrived at this point in my life. After all, we are who we are and we believe what we believe in large part not just because of our inherited genetic traits, but also because of the various events, both good and bad, that we experience throughout our lives.

My story is not so different from millions of others, possibly even yours. I was born and raised in small-town America. I would most certainly classify the town of my upbringing as a "Joe Six-Pack town." The focus and demeanor of the town was what I would consider relatively normal for a town of its size. Most people enjoyed high school sports, chatting it up over a cup of coffee at the local diner, as well as enjoying more than a couple of beers on the weekends—or any other day of the week, for that matter.

Like many Americans, alcohol consumption became a normal part of our lives and of the culture of our town. People drank, partied, and did the types of things that go along with that type of life-style, oftentimes regretting the events of the night before.

By most standards, I was raised in a relatively happy household. Growing up, I was surrounded by family and friends that cared for me and wanted nothing but the best for my life. Smiles and laughter were commonplace in our household. Alcohol consumption was commonplace as well, but for the most part, while I was young, I was never exposed to any of the negative side effects associated with drinking alcohol. It wouldn't be until later that I would realize the downside that alcohol can play in an individual's life.

But there was another side to the environment in which I was raised. It was a side that I always felt more comfortable with. It was a side of my life that always felt more safe and secure. It was the part of my upbringing that I enjoyed the most.

My parents took my sister and me to church on a regular basis. We would go to church on Sundays, sing hymns, and learn about God and His son, Jesus Christ. Everything about this aspect of my life felt lighter, happier, more genuine, and especially more natural to my spirit.

In church, we memorized Bible verses and learned the stories of the Bible, including those about Jesus's miracles. It was in these formative years of my life that I believe that the seeds of my faith were planted. I believe that it was due to this strong foundation that was built at a young age that I was able to return to Christ later in my life, but it would take the better part of two decades before doing so.

Bad Choices

Things in my life began to take a turn for the worse later in adolescence. For many, adolescence can be a rough time. The reason for this is that it is at this time in our lives that we are experiencing significant changes that oftentimes can leave us with feelings of confusion. Major transitions in our lives can lead to searching for answers, and oftentimes with few solutions. It can be a confusing and frustrating time or many. Not to mention, it is at this age that we desperately want to fit in with the crowd.

It was in my senior year of high school when I began to venture down a darker path. As mentioned before, alcohol consumption was a normal part of life where I grew up, and it was considered almost as a rite of passage for teens in high school to take up drinking alcohol and partying on a regular basis. I never stopped to question the morality of it all. It all seemed so normal. For the most part, the adults in the community turned a blind eye to our juvenile delinquency and passed it off as kids being kids. Most felt that there was no harm being done.

I had always considered myself to possess adequate social skills. I was never painfully shy. I made friends easily and volunteered regularly to answer questions in the classroom, but despite having some success on the field of play, like most teenage boys, I was still shy when it came to girls. I quickly realized that after a couple of beers, I began to loosen up a bit. It didn't take long for the nervousness to dissipate and for me to feel more comfortable talking to my peers of the opposite sex.

Before I knew it, alcohol had become my "social lubricant." I began to associate a feeling of comfort in social situations with the consumption of alcohol. But like many, what started off as good-natured fun started to take a negative toll on my life.

Eventually, alcohol consumption would evolve into something that was done to escape the realities and stresses of life. Nobody ever thinks when they take that first drink that they will ever abuse alcohol or possibly even develop a problem, and I was no different.

Finding My Way

Like so many others, upon leaving high school, I felt uncertain and anxious about what my future held. My family didn't have a lot of money, and I wasn't sure how my college tuition was going to be paid.

Also, without high school sports, I had suddenly lost my sense of identity. I began to experience uncertainty about who I was and where I was heading. I also began to struggle with my level of self-worth. I had always been known as the wrestler and football player, but after graduating high school, I wasn't sure as to where to find my significance. My life needed a change. After carefully weighing my options, I made the choice to enlist in the United States Air Force.

Initially the military was great. I enjoyed the regimented schedule, the discipline, the clean living, and the Spartan lifestyle of basic training. I embraced the structure and felt the sense of purpose and self-worth that I had been missing since moving on from high school.

But soon after basic training, the frustration and disillusionment that had begun to emerge toward the end of high school returned. I had a nagging sense that something was missing, but I couldn't seem to put my finger on what it was.

I was homesick, stressed, and lonely while away, so I did the one thing that had always seemed to be the solution when faced with a hardship. I turned to alcohol.

Drinking alcohol wasn't a problem in regard to my duties or other military-related obligations, but when the boys and I had a chance to get out on the weekends, we held nothing back.

I was never physically addicted to alcohol, but I definitely abused it on a regular basis, oftentimes drinking to the point of blackout, constantly trying to numb and distract myself from the reality of being away from home. Alcohol had now become my go-to coping mechanism. I began to find that any time I faced a challenge or was forced to deal with a hardship, I would find my escape in alcohol. After four years in the United States Air Force, I had earned an honorable discharge, and once again, it was on to the next chapter of my life.

The College Life

In the months between leaving the military and starting college, the stresses of life continued to build. During my first semester of college, I was taking a general education health class, at which time we were learning about the havoc that stress can wreak on the body. We filled out a survey to determine our stress level according to the various stressors that we were currently facing at that time in our lives.

At the time, I was confronted with a number of challenging situations including the transition from military to civilian life, starting college, the loss of my grandmother (paternal) and my grandfather (maternal) within a few months of one another, the divorce of my parents after twenty-six years of marriage, and a breakup with my longtime girlfriend. Everything seemed to be going wrong all at once, and I felt like my world was falling apart.

Upon finishing the survey, the results revealed that I had such a multitude of stressors that it was determined to be detrimental to my health. I remember thinking to myself, "Oh well, what can I do about it?" My mind-set was always to put my head down and soldier on. The real problem, however, was that I wasn't exactly sure how to deal with these stressors.

In college, alcohol continued to be my crutch for coping with all the chaos in my life. I justified it by saying, "This is what I'm supposed to do in college." But in reality, I knew that I was taking things too far. I began going out three to four nights per week, but despite my overly active social life, I was able to maintain a high GPA and fulfill all my academic responsibilities. I point this out not in order to be boastful, but rather because my life had not been impaired by alcohol to the point that I felt that it was a problem. In many cases, this is how an individual justifies to themselves the use of drugs, alcohol, or any other coping mechanism.

Despite being able to handle the academic rigors of college, I couldn't help but feel a growing sense of frustration, disillusionment, and despair. It was as though there was a dark cloud hanging over my head, but I wasn't sure why. It felt like my emotional pain was building like a pressure cooker. The problem was that I was still turning to alcohol to serve as my release valve, an attempt that was failing miserably.

I still maintained my religious beliefs, but my faith low on my list of priorities. My mind-set was that I didn't have room in my life for God and that I would return to Him when I was able to straighten things out.

The Real World

With college graduation came the anxiety of starting a new chapter of my life and entering the "real world." It was time to start a career in teaching. After a year of substitute teaching, I was fortunate enough to land a full-time position teaching history.

I was excited to finally be in a position where, financially, I would no longer be struggling to make ends meet. I could finally live a more stable life. But I was not prepared for the stresses that came from teaching full-time while also taking on coaching responsibilities, as well as serving as the student council advisor. It was not unusual for my day to be filled with school-related activities seven days a week, oftentimes putting in fourteen hour days (anyone who thinks that a teacher's day lasts from seven to three is sadly mistaken).

At that time, I would joke that I wasn't sure why I paid rent since I was hardly ever at my apartment.

After my first four years, things hadn't slowed down much. I was still carrying a full load of responsibilities that didn't leave much time for relaxing or a social life. But when I would get some time away from work, it was normally filled with trying to unwind, usually with my old acquaintance, alcohol.

I found myself putting on weight, feeling extremely unhealthy, lethargic, and generally unhappy. I was frustrated, lost, and, overall, depressed. The uncertainty in my life came from the continuing sense of discontent and, most frustratingly of all, not knowing why. After all, I was making a decent living, and although I was extremely busy, everyone is. So why did I feel so unhappy?

The void in my soul persisted. I did my best to try to fill it with anything I could get my hands on—food, alcohol, and other meaningless endeavors. I was living in that dark place where many others dwell. I was broken by life, but wasn't sure how to get fixed. It wasn't as if I had hit rock bottom by most standards, but at the same time, I was far from being happy.

I believe that this is the most dangerous place of all to find yourself because you do not feel desperate enough to make the changes necessary, yet you certainly aren't living the life that you had always envisioned for yourself. What I didn't realize is that my life would soon take a significant turn for the better.

A "Fortunate" Series of Events

And then one day things began to change. After a series of what seemed like unfortunate events, I thought to myself, "Here we go again, why do these things always seem to happen to me?" It began when my coaching career came to an abrupt end unexpectedly. This was followed by being forced to move out of my apartment due to a new downstairs neighbor who thought because he didn't have to get up early and go to work, it wouldn't matter if he had friends over every night of the week and partied until the early hours of the morning. These events were followed up by a stressful breakup with my girlfriend. Once again my life was at a crossroads.

At that time, I felt overwhelmed by the situation, but looking back now, I realize that all these things were a blessing in disguise. Suddenly, I experienced a considerable increase in the amount of free time in my life. I knew in my heart that it was time to make the changes that were long overdue. It was then that I decided to genuinely reconnect with my Heavenly Father.

Since my teenage years, I had gradually drifted further from the beliefs of my upbringing, and although I still held a belief in God, I felt as though I had grown distant from Him. I still had a longing in my heart, but I kept telling myself that once I got married and settled down, I would begin to reestablish that connection. Little did I know that by neglecting to reconnect with God, I was inadvertently preventing myself from living the amazing life that he had in store for me.

The Awakening

I decided to begin reading my Bible on a daily basis, nothing extreme, but I began to read five pages per day. I wanted to keep my daily readings brief in order to allow myself time to digest and process what I had read. It was at this time that I also began to pray in a more genuine, devout fashion. What I mean by this is that I would literally get down on my knees and ask God to show me and make evident the way in which He wanted me to live my life.

I also began to express gratitude more and consciously thank Him for what He had already done for me in my life. I mean, let's face it, I wasn't anywhere close to where I wanted to be, but things definitely could have been worse. As a matter of fact, when looking back on my life, I can see times when God was already actively involved in my life even though I wasn't consciously aware of it.

I began to ask the Heavenly Father for His divine guidance. I knew that He had a plan for my life and that if I would serve Him, I could live the life that I always knew was possible.

Another of the most important steps that I had taken was that I began to abstain from the use of alcohol. I remember feeling like a hypocrite when I would warn my students about the perils of drugs and alcohol, and yet every weekend, I was dumping gallons of alcohol down my throat. I began to focus on trying to improve my life in all aspects: mind, body, and especially spirit.

I am not being overly dramatic when I say that I began to see changes occur in my life immediately. It didn't take long before I had bought my own house in the mountains. It was a small home on three acres of land in a secluded area. This was one of the greatest blessings to have ever been bestowed upon me. What happened next was nothing short of a transcendental experience, much like that spoken of by authors such as Ralph Waldo Emerson and Henry David Thoreau.

For the next year of my life, I began to spend a lot of time in solitude. I would sit in nature and contemplate the deeper questions in life. I would ask myself questions such as, "What does God want from me? What is my purpose on this earth, and how do people truly achieve happiness?"

I would focus on these questions, and allow my mind to process them. Through God's divine blessings, I began to come up with a surprising amount of answers. I began to realize that the answers to all of life's questions can be found within us, by searching our very own souls. And with the elimination of alcohol from my life, my mind now processed information more clearly than ever. I started to feel like I was beginning to see the grand scheme of things.

Like many throughout history, I had made a profound connection with God in the wilderness. When alone in nature, one has no distractions from the outside world. I feel it is at this time that we can hear God speak to our soul. I have had some of my greatest epiphanies while alone in nature.

Guided by the Divine

It wasn't until recently in my life that I began to appreciate the struggles that the Lord has blessed me with throughout my life. We all start off in life with various levels of talent and ability. For me, I always had a great sense of curiosity and was able to verbalize and articulate on paper relatively well.

I've dealt with challenges and stress, just as every other human being on earth, but what I didn't understand fully until recently was that each one of these chapters in my life served a purpose. Throughout the years, during each stage of my life, my Heavenly Father was molding me into the person that He wanted me to become. I was acquiring skills and knowledge that would be essential later in life. Despite the fact that I wasn't always comfortable, and sometimes I even questioned why I was being forced to endure certain situations, looking back, I am extremely grateful because now I see that His Divine Hand was guiding me all along. I now realize that through these hardships, He was shaping me to become the person that I needed to be. Throughout the years, He has allowed me to develop invaluable skills and characteristics that will benefit me for the rest of my life.

For example, throughout my wrestling career, I was able to develop a great understanding of the absolute necessity of setting goals to serve as a road map for life and in order to offer direction so that you know what you are striving toward. Wrestling also taught me to work as hard as humanly possible in order to accomplish those goals.

But perhaps the most important lesson that I was able to take away from my wrestling career was how to overcome loss and the disappointment of falling short of what you've set out to accomplish, despite your best efforts.

During my time served in the United States Air Force, I was able to learn how to think methodically and in a logical manner. Through my training as a mechanic, I was taught to identify, troubleshoot, and repair a problem or malfunction. Later on in life, I found myself applying this same methodology to various aspects of my life. This methodic, logical way of thinking has helped me tremendously to overcome various challenges, as well as sort through the difficulties of life.

Throughout my teaching career, my development was twofold. First, I was able to attain a greater understanding of the world through the study of significant historical events and people. I was able to extract life lessons and attain an understanding of various cultures, as well as the cause and effect of a multitude of events throughout history. I was able to attain a better understanding of the world.

By learning and teaching history, I was able to research significant individuals that had made tremendous contributions to mankind. I became aware of and fascinated by the various works of people such as the German monk Martin Luther, Mahatma Gandhi, Eleanor Roosevelt, and Winston Churchill. I was also able to learn about the various events that shaped the world in which we live today.

Not only was I able to learn about significant people and events, I was also able to learn about the various cultures and religions of the world. I was able to gain a better appreciation for my fellow man and how the various peoples of the world live their lives. Along with this came the studying of various sociological and psychological schools, theories, and concepts. Teaching allowed me to develop skills that are essential to a successful happy life such as planning and organization, as well as managing groups of people. I was able to develop the critical skill of ensuring that I was in the right mind-set each day so that I could do my job efficiently and effectively. As any teacher will attest, you have to be "on" at all times. If not, the class will eat you alive!

The second aspect of teaching that I have benefitted from tremendously is from a social perspective. Dealing with students each day allowed me to hone my skills and knowledge on so many levels. I was able to develop an understanding of people. Skills such as how to motivate and engage individuals, how to develop and maintain excitement and interest, how to gauge and assess learning and understanding, along with so many other benefits that are too many to mention, were all acquired through teaching. And now, being a teacher by profession, I am happy to say that I feel as though I can use the skills that I have acquired over the decades in order to help those in need.

I firmly believe that this is the reason that the Lord has blessed me with the trials and challenges that I have faced throughout my life. I can now look back on all these experiences with a great deal of gratitude and know that without these challenges, I would have missed out on a great deal of personal development.

Your Father Is Forging You

The reason that I tell you my story is not to brag about the challenges that I have overcome, nor is it in order to seek sympathy. But rather I tell you my story because before I was able to reconnect with the Lord, I was down and out. I was lost. I could barely stand to look at myself in the mirror. But by the grace of God, I found my way. Little by little, I was able to find and create the life that I had always dreamed of. I have finally been able to find the happiness and fulfillment that I had been searching for my entire life, and the good news is that no matter where you are in life, you too can experience that same kind of joy!

Believe it or not, as you are reading this, you too possess the ability necessary to create the same kind of change in your life. Looking back now, I realize that all the trials and tribulations that I had suffered through were a tremendous blessing. I firmly believe that I was subjected to hardships and then shown the path to salvation so that I could then bring the knowledge that I had discovered to others who are going through many of the same types of struggles.

Oftentimes, when going through struggles, like me, many people, only focus on survival, and after coming through the other side, they're just glad they've made it. But the truth is that up to this point in your life, your Father in heaven has been and is molding you into the person that He wants you to become, even though you may not realize it. As a matter of fact, sometimes the most extreme difficulties prove to be the ones that are the most beneficial to developing our character. Just as the blacksmith must heat and pound the metal in order to forge his work, you too must be exposed to extreme heat and pressure in order for you to be formed into the person that you must become. I firmly believe that if you were to take a good, hard look at your life, you would see that all the challenges that you have been faced with and overcome in your life have served a purpose. You have no doubt grown stronger and become better as a result. It is imperative to realize that God has subjected you to these hardships so that you can develop the necessary skills and characteristics to fulfill your destiny.

I Want to Help You!

I believe that my story, minus a few details, is not so different from millions of others. I too was extremely unhappy. I too had found myself suffering, but frustratingly enough, I didn't know why.

I'd always been fascinated by the human mind and how it worked. I've also always been fascinated by successful individuals and the characteristics that determined whether a person would become happy and successful or not.

I also held a firm belief in the fact that anyone, and I mean anyone, could become successful and, more importantly, happy if they truly desired to be. I believed that it was simply a matter of figuring out a few key components in order to create a life full of happiness.

In 1 Corinthians 7:25, the apostle Paul states, "But the Lord in his mercy has given me wisdom that can be trusted, and I will share it with you." Paul was stating that the Lord had allowed him to discover important knowledge that he felt God wanted him to share with the world.

Along that same train of thought, I believe that the Lord has blessed me by answering my prayers and enlightening me in regard to the necessary steps in finding happiness. I've taken it upon myself to create a guide that will allow you to create a life of happiness and fulfillment because like many, I've seen the dark times, and after years of struggle and strife, I've found happiness. In turn, I want to help others find happiness as well. I want to save people the time and spare them from the trial and error that is oftentimes required in order to create the changes that many desire for their life.

To Be Happy Is a Universal Desire

It makes me feel both sad and frustrated to look around and see so many people lost, like I once was. So many people today are suffering, and yet I know that it doesn't have to be so.

As a matter of fact, it is my firm belief that if you were to ask any random person on the street what it is that they want most in life, the majority would answer simply, "To be happy."

And yet I find it very ironic that despite the fact that virtually every individual on earth possesses a strong desire to be happy, everywhere I look, I see people who are quite the opposite. The truth of the matter is that most people today are not only unhappy, but rather downright miserable.

As mentioned before, I too was once miserable like so many others today, and I too, like so many others, desperately wanted to be happy. The problem was that just like most people, I wasn't quite sure how to acquire happiness.

Getting Off Course

Something that is oftentimes overlooked is that most people do not experience a sudden traumatic event that throws them off course and forces them down a dark path in life. Rather, what happens to most people is that they simply look around one day and come to the realization that their life has not turned out the way that they had envisioned. They realize that they're frustrated, unhappy, and unfulfilled, and yet they're not even sure how they arrived at this station in life.

The truth of the matter is that getting off course is much easier than most people realize. Even if a person is only off course by a small amount in one or two areas of their life, over time, this can lead to an individual straying and finding themselves far from their destination, and this, in turn will keep them from the life that they truly wish for themselves.

For example, in most cases, an individual doesn't suddenly put on fifty pounds in a matter of days or even weeks, but rather it happens over a period of months and years. The weight comes on so gradually that one doesn't even notice. Sure, maybe those pants fit a little tighter, but we find a way to rationalize it in our minds. We tell ourselves that our pants must be shrinking, or maybe we have put on a pound or two, but it's nothing to worry about.

Or maybe an individual begins to hang around the wrong crowd during their teenage years. They begin to get into trouble because they're being influenced negatively by their peers. Years down the road, they find themselves with a criminal record, far from the life that they thought they would be living as an adult. These examples are common.

In the world of navigation, there exists something known as Atomic Time. Atomic Time refers to a system designed to keep precise time throughout the globe. A series of four hundred atomic clocks are used to maintain the exact time throughout the world, and this time is so accurate that it will only deviate approximately one second every twenty million years (http://www.timeanddate.com/time/international-atomic-time.html)!

I know what you may be wondering, "Why is it so important to keep such accurate time?" That's a great question, and the answer is that it is vital in the realm of navigation both by sea and air to have extremely accurate time. The reason for this is that in order to calculate precise location and direction, the sun's position at a given time is used, along with latitude and longitude. Therefore, if the time is off even by a small increment, over time this will result in a vessel straying far off course. For example, if the time is off by only a few seconds, one could get off course and end up tens or even hundreds of miles from their desired location.

What does this have to do with you? This very same thing happens in many peoples' lives. They get off course in one area of life or another only by a small increment. It doesn't seem like a big deal to drink a couple beers every night or to have a late-night snack here and there, or maybe even to splurge a little when it comes to shopping, spending a couple hundred dollars on things that we don't really need. Or perhaps we're out running around with the wrong crowd, getting into a little trouble here and there. After a few weeks, months, or years we find ourselves far off course, nowhere near our desired destination. Getting off course can affect our lives financially, in our health, and even in our personal relationships.

If you've been off course, whether it be for a short period of time or perhaps longer, it's time to recalibrate your life. It's time to reset your "internal atomic clock" and get back on track. I promise you that once you set your course straight, you will notice the positive results almost immediately!

Desperation Opens the Door for Tragedy

In 1918, at the conclusion of the First World War, the Allied Powers emerged victorious. As could be expected, the victors wanted revenge for all the death and destruction that had occurred during the Great War. In turn, the Allies imposed an incredible price tag on their conquered opponents in the form of war reparations and various other punishments. But what the Allies did not realize is that what they were doing was inadvertently setting the stage for another larger, even more destructive conflict.

The German people found themselves not only conquered, but also humiliated, ashamed, depressed, and hopeless about their future. This led the Germans to become desperate for answers to their dire situation. They needed some sort of solution to their problems. Unfortunately none was in sight. These hopeless conditions created an ideal environment that would eventually give rise to one of the most maniacal dictators to have ever walked the face of the earth, Adolf Hitler.

Many people today pose the question, "How did the German people allow such an evil man to seize control of their nation?" The answer is simpler than it may seem. You see, the German people were so desperate and hopeless that despite Hitler not necessarily seeming like the best option *possible*, he was the best option *available*. He made promises to restore the German people to a life even better than before the war. He offered them a solution to what seemed like an unsolvable problem. Hitler was not only able to take advantage of the situation to seize power, but he would go on to wage war on a never-before-seen scale.

Just as in pre-World War II Germany, in today's world, we oftentimes see negativity seize control in people lives when they've become hopeless and desperate. When it seems as if all hope is lost and there is no solution or way out of a bad situation, negativity and sometimes even evil take over, for it is in these times that we are spiritually weak and most vulnerable. Oftentimes these situations can lead to depression, crime, and even substance abuse. The good news is that even if you've found yourself moving toward a negative path, it is not too late. You can still turn things around.

The Messy Garage Syndrome

Today many people are suffering from what I like to call "messy garage syndrome." Allow me to elaborate. A few years ago, I opened the door to my garage, and the sight that lay before me was utterly overwhelming and terrifying. I saw an old hammock, a few stacks of books, some materials from work, containers of "stuff," and many other random items that had accumulated and been stashed away since moving into our new house. I remember thinking to myself, "I don't even know where to begin," and quickly shutting the door.

I believe that this is the exact way that many people today feel about their life. Many of us have been faced with a multitude of issues and challenges throughout the years, which can become very overwhelming, and, as a result, are sometimes ignored and pushed aside for lack of a better solution. We oftentimes find ourselves doing our best to avoid dealing with the situation.

Unfortunately, this eventually brings us to a point in our lives where we find ourselves with a life full of issues that need to be and should be addressed and resolved, but by this point, they have been piling up for so long that we're not sure where to begin. The answer to this situation is simple, with one issue at a time.

The Worst Sinner

Saul despised Christians. As a matter of fact, he hated them. He hated Christians so badly that he even took it upon himself to hunt them down and persecute anyone that had the audacity to spread the Gospel that had been brought to earth by Jesus Christ. He despised early Christians to such an extent that he had even at times played a role in their execution.

And then something amazing happened. It occurred one day while Saul was traveling on the road to Damascus in order to hunt down more Christians, when he was stopped in his tracks by a blinding light. The book of Acts tells the story of Saul being surrounded by the light and hearing a voice that said, "Saul, Saul, why do you persecute me?" (Acts 9:4 NIV)

The voice that Saul heard that day was that of Jesus Christ Himself. Jesus sent Saul on to Damascus, where he would meet up with the disciple Ananias. It would be three days before Saul would regain his sight. Eventually he would change his name to Paul, and from that point forward, he would go on to become an apostle of the Lord, who would spread the word of God throughout the land and help establish the early church, as well as be credited with writing a significant portion of the New Testament.

In 1 Timothy 1:15–17 (NIV), Paul would say "Here is a trustworthy saying that deserves full acceptance: Christ Jesus came into the world to save sinners—*of whom I am the worst*. But for that very reason I was shown mercy so that in me, the worst of sinners, Christ Jesus might display his unlimited patience as an example for those who would believe on him and receive eternal life." (Italics added.)

Some may be left wondering, "Why would God select the self-proclaimed 'worst sinner' to go forth and do His work?"

That is a great question, but we must see the brilliance in God's divine plan. You see, God intentionally selected the worst sinner of all, a man who despised and hated Christians, to be the one to go into the world and perform some of the most significant work in the history of the church in order to display the extent of His unconditional love, as well as to prove that there is *no one* who is beyond saving.

Paul was the self-proclaimed worst sinner of all, and even he received the Lord's divine grace. Therefore, nobody is beyond the reach of God's salvation. This means that you and I too will receive the Lord's grace regardless of our mistakes of the past. The fact stands that God shows us His divine mercy and grace so that we too can go forth into the world and testify in His name and bring others to Him so that they may be saved. What an amazing blessing!

You Deserve to Be Happy!

One of the biggest problems that many are facing today is that they do not feel deserving of happiness for reasons that will be discussed on the following pages. Unfortunately, those who do not feel worthy of happiness will never find it. So let me just start by saying that you *must believe that you absolutely deserve to be happy*!

The wisdom necessary to create a happy life has been accessible for thousands of years. The secret to happiness is that it's not a secret at all. It's as simple as applying a few basic rules and principles to one's life. The reason that most people find themselves unhappy is because they are either unaware of or unwilling to apply this wisdom. The truth is that the path to happiness is not about money or wealth. As a matter of fact, a happy life can be created at no cost at all.

I am being sincere when I say that I genuinely believe that no matter who you are, where you're from, or how much you or your family is worth, you can and should be happy. And like I said before, you deserve it! It's time for you to create the life that you are not only searching for but are also desperately yearning for.

Happiness Can Become a Reality for You

As mentioned earlier, many people in this world today are lost. They aren't sure how they got lost or how to get unlost, but they know that they're not where they want to be.

And so I decided to write this book so that I may save those who read it from the years of suffering and the trial and error that I subjected myself to before finally finding my way. I feel as though it is our responsibility to pass on and share the wisdom that has been given to us through our various experiences in life.

I want this book to serve as your road map. It should be used to take you from being lost in the wilderness of life to the path that you truly want to be on, the path of righteousness and happiness.

But just like any map, it is useless to possess it unless it is put to good use. If I were to hand you a treasure map and you put it in your pocket, where it stayed for the rest of your life, the treasure would never be found or enjoyed. The same reigns true for the guidelines on the following pages. They must be used and applied.

As you are reading this now, your Heavenly Father is calling you to this path. It has been there your whole life, but like most people, you have become lost and have not been able to find it. Once you have discovered the path, I promise you that in a short time, you will begin to see positive changes unfold in your life.

As you read this book, I encourage you to mark pages, highlight passages, make notes in the margins, and refresh your memory when needed. Share this book with others. Offer them the gift of happiness as well.

I've written this book for those individuals who feel the same way that I felt just a few short years ago, those who feel stuck, hopeless, and trapped in a life that seems to have no meaning or purpose and yet are not sure how to create the changes that they desire.

Like I said, anyone from anywhere is capable of making these changes in their life. I just ask that you please keep an open mind and allow the process to develop and make positive changes in your life.

For it is my genuine belief that it is the desire of our Father in Heaven for us to live a happy life full of enjoyment while on this earth, serving and glorifying Him. I can show you the path, but it is up to you whether or not walk on it. I firmly believe that if you follow the steps laid out before you in this book, you will have the ability to live the life that you've always dreamed of!

STEP 1

Make the Choice

"This is where your inspiration is found."

Choice: The Blessing that Shapes Your Life

Have you ever found yourself feeling frustrated with life but uncertain as to how to change? As previously mentioned, the initial answer is to take things one step at a time. In doing so, the first step that is absolutely essential in the transformation of your life is to simply make the choice. Before you begin to think that this solution may seem overly simplified, be honest with yourself. Have you ever truly in your heart made up your mind to take action in order to create the change that you so desperately desire in your life?

I ask you to take a minute and ask yourself, "Do I want to go on living unhappy and frustrated, or do I want to do what is necessary to make the changes that will allow me to live a life of happiness and fulfillment?" It is important to consciously decide which path you wish to walk in life.

The truth of the matter is that life is a series of choices. Each one of us is faced with hundreds, if not thousands, of choices to make each day. Obviously some decisions carry more weight than others, but the quality and outcome of a person's life are a culmination of the decisions that were made throughout their journey.

Each time we come to a fork in the road of life, we are choosing an event that is ultimately going to affect the quality of our life. The impact of most of these decisions is miniscule. Obviously choosing whether you wear your blue shirt or green to work on a particular day probably won't have a tremendous effect on your overall quality of life, but it is a veritable fact that some of the most significant times in your life will be when you are faced with an important decision to make.

The concept of the power of choice is absolutely essential to grasp prior to embarking on your journey of transformation and improving the overall quality of your life. Most people have the misconception that the amount of happiness and success that a person enjoys or is capable of acquiring is determined by the amount of good breaks and good luck that they will experience throughout their life. This simply is not true. That is precisely why it is imperative that you realize the significance of and the opportunities that lie in the blessing of choice.

It is important for you to understand that life is not a matter of good luck or bad. It's not a matter of getting all the breaks or none. None of that matters. What matters the most is the decisions that you make each and every day.

The most exciting thing about this notion is that if this is in fact true and the level of happiness that you will experience throughout your life is determined by the quality of the choices that you make, then this means that the level of happiness that you will or will not enjoy is completely and entirely up to you!

An Amazing Blessing

You may be wondering why it is that I continue to refer to the freedom to choose as a blessing. This concept is an integral component in attaining happiness. What I mean is that it is a blessing that has been bestowed upon us by our Heavenly Father.

You see, our Heavenly Father, in His infinite power and wisdom, could impose His will upon us and force us to live according to what aligns with His divine will. But through His infinite love and grace, He has given us the blessing to make our own choices in life and, in turn, has put us in complete control of our own destiny. His divine hand will never force us to make any decision. At times He may try to offer us direction by speaking to our hearts or through another method of persuasion, but ultimately He allows the choice to rest in our hands alone. Obviously there will be times when we make poor decisions, but our Father will allow us to choose, nonetheless, and then live with the consequences, whether good or bad.

I certainly do not want you to confuse what I'm saying with the notion that we have the ability to choose our circumstance. Circumstance, whether good or bad, is an element of our lives that is oftentimes out of our control.

Many people are born or forced into circumstances and situations that are completely not of their own doing. But although you may find yourself in less than ideal circumstances and whether or not you will take the appropriate steps necessary in order to improve your situation are two completely different things. *The power to change one's station in life is what comes with the blessing of choice.*

You Are Powerful Beyond Measure

The mistake that most people tend to make is looking at their situation with a feeling of helplessness, as if they have absolutely nowhere to turn and no way out. When faced with these types of challenges, it's important to realize that you are not the only person to have ever been handed unfortunate circumstances, and you certainly won't be the last.

But if you feel that your life is in need of a change, then it's up to you to make the decision and take the initial steps to get on the path to the life in which you wish to create

As author Napoleon Hill stated in his timeless classic *Think and Grow Rich*, "You are the master of your own destiny... You can make your life what you want it to be."

The Most Important Decision of Your Life is about to be Made

If you've purchased this book, then there is something about your life that you are not happy about. The areas of discontent vary from person to person, but the ultimate goal, which is a life full of happiness and fulfillment, does not.

Many of us tend to only look at our immediate future, but I want you to take a minute and imagine yourself five or ten years down the road, continuing on the path that you are currently on. It is almost certain that things are not likely to improve unless you decide to take action.

So therefore, I implore you, take responsibility for your life, make the choice, and take the steps necessary to get on the path and create the life that you have always dreamed of.

Stop Waiting for the Perfect Wave

Oftentimes we have a vision of what our ideal life would entail. Maybe we see this type life as something that we probably could never and will never attain.

We sometimes tell ourselves, "Someday when the circumstances are right, I'm going to do this or that." The problem lies in the fact that when we think about the pursuit of these goals and our ideal life, we sometimes feel as though it will have to wait until the time is right. What we must realize is that life is full of twists and turns, ups and downs. Therefore, if we sit back and wait until the "time is right," we will never even get started with the pursuit of the life of our dreams.

The situation is similar to that of a surfer waiting for the "perfect wave." If a surfer sits adrift in the ocean on his surfboard waiting for the perfect wave, the chances are that they will be sitting there all day bobbing up and down, floating aimlessly in the water.

You must realize that the conditions of your life will never be perfect, but if you make the decision to take action, you will begin to see gradual changes that will lead you to a life of happiness.

Are You Truly Living?

One of my all-time favorite movies is the 1995 blockbuster *Braveheart*. To those who are unfamiliar with this movie, it is based on the life of a man who lived in the highlands of Scotland during the late thirteen and early fourteenth century by the name of William Wallace. Wallace was a man who held deep personal convictions about life and the value of living free from subjugation. And he was willing to fight to the death if need be for what he truly believed in.

I distinctly remember when I first saw the film. One line in particular that really reverberated with me was during a scene in which Wallace has been captured and is being asked to submit to the oppressive King Edward I of England. If Wallace would submit, it was likely that he would be set free and literally could have saved his life. The problem was that in doing so, Wallace would be forced to give up his freedom and sacrifice everything that he stood for.

In the film, Wallace's reply to the request was not just a simple "no," but rather when it is made evident that he may live if he relents, he profoundly states, "Every man dies, not every man really lives."

I remember that upon hearing that line, it really struck a chord with me. I remember asking myself, "Am I truly living?"

I came to the realization that in today's world, many people are not truly living, but rather merely existing. Many are simply enduring a life of monotony and meaningless pursuits rather than feeling excited and passionate about life. As a result, their lives are lacking of any real substance.

It was at that point that I resolved to truly begin to live life to the fullest and not just merely exist. Oftentimes when we hear people speak of living life to the fullest, images of bungee jumping and skydiving come to mind. But on the contrary, although those are perfectly fine endeavors if that is what you choose to do, what I mean by living life to the fullest is pursuing meaningful goals that bring a sense of significance and genuine joy to one's life.

I believe that in order to live life to the fullest, one must take the talents and abilities that have been bestowed upon them by their Creator and utilize them to their fullest extent in order to maximize their potential, all the while glorifying their Heavenly Father in the process. By living this way, I believe that a person can truly get the most out of life and avoid living life in monotony and frustration.

I urge you to ask yourself, are you truly living, or are you merely existing? If your answer is the latter, then it's time to take action and make a change. There's no reason that you who are reading this book at this moment cannot get excited about life! As a matter of fact, while you're reading this very passage, you should feel a quickening of the pulse and a fire igniting in your stomach!

Acknowledge Impermanence

One day during school, the administration held a faculty meeting in order to recognize and honor the teachers on staff that had accumulated over twenty-five years of teaching. I was currently in my eighth year and remember thinking to myself how surprisingly fast it had gone.

At the end of the meeting, I met on the way out one of the teachers who had been recognized for his thirty years of service. Our eyes met, and I said to him, "I'll bet it doesn't seem like thirty years, does it?"

He looked at me and shook his head in disbelief and replied, "Bill, you can't imagine how fast it's gone!"

On my way home that day, I contemplated the notion of a thirty-year teaching career and also thought about how quickly the past eight years had gone by. I was thinking about the fact that time had passed so quickly and questioned as to why it seemed to be so. I realized that sometimes we get so caught up in life and so accustomed to our "daily grind" year in and year out that before we know it, we look around and the better part of a few decades has passed us by.

This was a startling revelation. I remember thinking, "I can't afford to waste another day going through the motions and not making the most out of this life." I knew that I needed to stop spinning my wheels and take the reins to ensure that I made this life worth remembering.

In the book of Psalms, the Bible states that our lives are but a breath. In the book of James, it compares life to a "mist or vapor."

Oftentimes our lives are filled with statements such as "maybe someday" or "when I get time I'm going to (*fill in the blank*)." It's imperative for us to realize that none of us are immortal. It is a fact that someday you and I will leave this earth. I'm certainly not saying this in a morbid sense, but rather in a matter-of-fact manner.

Our lives are going to pass us by more quickly than we think. Again I'm not saying this to instill fear but rather to instill a sense of urgency. I hope that you and I both live long lives, but if we're not careful, by the time we enter into the twilight of our years, there's a chance that we could look back and be disappointed with the way that we've lived our lives. Nothing brings more sadness than neglecting to act on all the things that we should have done and, for one reason or another, failing to pursue the goals that were in our hearts. So therefore, I implore you, do not allow this to occur in your life. Do not look back with regret. You must take action now!

Stop Losing Time

The highly regarded life coach Jim Rohn once stated, "Time is more valuable than money." Mr. Rohn could not have been more correct in this statement because money can be recovered, but once time is lost, it is gone forever. Each second that passes by without moving forward toward the life that you desire is a second that you can never get back.

Small Decisions Equal Big Changes

Oftentimes the most effective way to create the changes that we want to see in our lives is through the small decisions that we make each day.

As mentioned in the introduction of this book, we oftentimes feel overwhelmed by the very thought of trying to "clean up" our lives. To many, the task seems so daunting that they feel intimidated, or maybe even aren't sure where to begin.

But if you can identify a few areas of your life in which you would like to experience change and then begin to make small decisions in the right direction each day toward addressing those specific areas, you will begin to notice the positive results in a short period of time.

Don't Be Paralyzed by Fear

On June 6, 1944, the United States, along with its World War II Allies, launched the largest land invasion in modern history on the beaches of Normandy in an event that would become known as the D-Day Invasion. Months of planning went into the invasion, diversions were set, and the Allies planned on throwing everything they had at their German foes in the assault. This was literally going to be a do-or-die situation.

One aspect of the landings that is oftentimes overlooked due to the sheer magnitude of the attack is that the Nazis had set up a tremendous amount of fortifications along the beach in anticipation of a forthcoming invasion. Although Hitler and his comrades were expecting the invasion to come further up the beach, they spared no expense in setting up defenses—this included barbed wire, Teller mines, pillboxes, concrete bunkers, and Belgian gates (a heavy steel fence that took a considerable amount of explosives to remove), among other obstacles—all along the entire beach.

In order for the invasion to be successful, it was absolutely essential that these obstacles were cleared before the main invasion force was to land. The fortifications would continue to be cleared throughout the invasion. This task was left up to a courageous group of men known as the Naval Combat Demolition Units, which was a precursor to the Navy SEALs. In the film *Navy Seals: Their Untold Story*, Ken Reynolds, a member of the unit, when speaking of clearing the beaches stated that some men were so frozen by fear that they were simply unable to move from behind the barrier on the beach in which they had taken cover. Reynolds and his fellow demolition men, following strict orders, would set an explosive charge and then move on to the next obstacle. The resulting explosion was of tremendous magnitude, and as Reynolds would say, some men were unable to move away from the detonation due to the paralysis caused by their extreme fear. It goes without saying that unfortunately many never made it off the beach that day.

The fact of the matter was that the men felt safer hunkered down behind a barrier, even though they risked the possibility of being blown up, than they did taking the chance to move forward and risk being hit by enemy fire. As they sat petrified behind the barrier, with time running out before the detonation, the chance of their survival became miniscule.

The reason that I'm mentioning this story is that oftentimes in life, just as in the D-Day Invasion, many people find themselves with the same type of mental lapse, which results from being paralyzed by fear. Most times they're not in a life-threatening situation, such as the men involved in the D-Day Invasion, but their situation may seem just as terrifying, nonetheless.

It could be someone who is facing a tremendous amount of debt, a health crisis, or some other type of mental or psychological challenge. Regardless of the situation, you cannot afford to allow yourself to be paralyzed by fear. It is imperative that you continue to make progress and move forward toward the life that you envision for yourself. The most detrimental mistake that you could make is to remain stationary.

Utilize Momentum

We've all heard Isaac Newton's famous first law of motion, which states, "An object in motion tends to stay in motion." Despite the fact that Newton's law is referring to celestial bodies, this scientific law can also be applied to an individual's life. If you can approach each day with the right mind-set and decide that you are *not* going to smoke that cigarette or drink that beer or that you *will* go for a one-mile walk or read five pages of the Bible, you will begin to see progress as these positive decisions continue to build and gain momentum with each passing day. As your progress continues to grow, so will your motivation, and *nothing serves as better motivation than results*!

The more that you progress and see positive results, the more you will be inspired. In turn, the more inspired you are, the more motivated you will be, and your life will continue to move forward in a positive direction.

Before you know it, you will have lost those stubborn pounds or have read nearly the entire Bible, or perhaps you've finished that college degree that you've been putting off for years.

I urge you to stop simply existing through life and start living your life! If you continue to build momentum by making the right decisions each day, someday you will look back and say to yourself with a smile, "I did it!

Making Tough Choices: Challenge Yourself!

One of my favorite individuals from history is none other than the renowned US president Theodore Roosevelt, also known simply as TR. If you are unfamiliar with Teddy's story, it goes something like this.

Born in 1858, Teddy came from a family of wealth and prestige. But despite his privileged background, Teddy was a sickly boy who suffered from debilitating asthma. As a matter of fact, Teddy's ailment was so severe that he spent a significant amount of time bedridden throughout his youth.

It would have been easy for Teddy to simply accept his frailty and spend the rest of his life being pampered and catered to. Certainly men with less resolve would have simply accepted their illness and done that very thing, but that simply was not the character of Teddy Roosevelt. As a matter of fact, had Teddy relented to his illness, we probably wouldn't be talking about him today.

Rather, Teddy became sick and tired of being sick and tired and resolved to do something about it. Teddy decided to embrace what he referred to as the "strenuous life." He began training his mind and body until he became a force to be reckoned with who simply would not take no for an answer.

Teddy also began to challenge himself through various endeavors. After being homeschooled for most of his youth, he enrolled at the prestigious Harvard University. At Harvard, Teddy participated in some of the school's most strenuous activities, including boxing, rowing, and wrestling. Teddy challenged himself academically as well and would go on to graduate *magna cum laude.*

Upon graduation, many expected Teddy to go into business and make a comfortable living. Although that may have been a more convenient choice, Teddy decided to commit his tenacious energy to politics. He was determined to attack and clean up the vast corruption that was plaguing New York City, as well as the entire nation. Although many thought that the young Roosevelt was out of his mind, there was no challenge that Teddy believed he could not overcome. Teddy was once quoted as saying, "*Believe you can, and you're halfway there.*"

And so Teddy went on with his life, embracing the strenuous life. He continued to make the tough choices that would allow him to continue challenging himself each day.

At one point, Teddy even resigned from his position as the assistant secretary of the navy in order to join the military and test his mettle in the Spanish-American War.

At the Battle of San Juan Hill, Teddy led his men in a charge that would earn him nationwide acclaim for his bravery and courage in battle. The future president would go on to become the only commander in chief to be awarded the Medal of Honor, the nation's highest military honor.

Teddy became the hero of the Spanish-American War for his actions on the field of battle, and his notoriety led to his nomination as vice-president under William McKinley.

Shortly thereafter, McKinley was killed by an assassin's bullet, making TR the youngest president in US history at the age of forty-two.

Teddy would go on to have a tremendous career and life by continually making the decision to challenge himself in order to overcome insurmountable odds.

When it was all said and done, TR could list among his accomplishments thirty-five books, nine spoken languages, a Nobel Peace Prize, thousands of acres of preserved natural habitat, taking on the big business leaders of his day (earning him the nickname the "Trustbuster") while also helping to improve relationships between business owners and workers, improving workers' rights, and becoming credited as one of America's most popular presidents of all time.

Entire books have been written about the endeavors of this great man, and when I would learn and teach about such men, it reinforced my belief that there truly is such a thing as destiny. When you see an individual who seems to come along at just the right place and just the right time, it seems as though there is no other explanation.

I sincerely believe that despite the hardships that Teddy faced as a young boy, it was due to his conscious decision to challenge himself and not always take the easy way that allowed him to accomplish such amazing feats and fulfill his destiny. Had Teddy done what most thought that he would do and played it safe throughout his life, history would have missed out on one of its truly great individuals.

So what does this have to do with you, you may ask? The answer is everything because just like Teddy, you too have an amazing life in store for you, but first you must make the tough decisions and be willing to challenge yourself.

Fulfill Your Destiny

It is my firm belief that each of us has a destiny or purpose in our lives that we are meant to accomplish before leaving this earth. But unless we are willing to make the right decisions and have the courage and wherewithal like Teddy Roosevelt to challenge ourselves and embrace the "strenuous life," we risk allowing our destiny to go unfulfilled. Not all of us are destined to win the Medal of Honor or become president of the United States, but our destinies are no less significant, nonetheless.

Perhaps you are destined to raise a happy, successful child or to start a nonprofit organization that will go on to benefit thousands, or maybe it is to fulfill another dream that has been living in your heart.

Focus on the Why

One important element in our pursuit of a happy life that is important to keep in mind is to focus on the why. What I mean by this is that so many times in life, people tend to get caught up on the what.

For example, they may say to themselves, "I feel very anxious." The fact that they have identified the way that they feel is great, but it will not help to resolve the problem. By focusing on the why, they will be able to analyze the problem and break down the reasons for feeling anxious and then take the necessary action in order to remedy the situation.

So instead of focusing on the fact that they feel anxious, they should focus on why they feel anxious. In this particular case, it may be due to an upcoming exam later in the week. By not focusing on the feeling of being anxious but rather why they feel anxious, the individual can then take the appropriate steps necessary to relieve their feelings of anxiety such as ensuring adequate study time, leading to a feeling of relaxed confidence.

Far too many times in life, people get hung up on the *what*, which leads to the persistence of the problem, rather than the *why*, which leads to the solution and, ultimately, improvement.

Choose to Be Happy

Far too many times, people tend to think that happiness is based on circumstance. The truth of the matter is that a person can be happy in any situation. That's right, you can be happy right now at this very instant!

Don't get me wrong. I'm certainly not implying that everything is currently perfect in your life or that there isn't anything that you would change if you could. I'm not suggesting that you have plenty of money, the house of your dreams, or maybe the relationship that you've always desired. But regardless of the situation that you are currently in, it is up to you to decide whether or not you will be happy.

It has been said that "no matter how much you have, there is someone in this world who is happy with less." Abraham Lincoln once famously said, "Most folks are as happy as they make up their minds to be."

Choosing to be happy can make all the difference in the world. I think that we can all attest to the fact that we would rather spend time around someone who is happy rather than someone who is always suffering from the doldrums. The path to happiness lies in your decision to be happy and in following the steps laid out before you on the following pages.

Make It a Ride to Remember

So again I reiterate, a concept that it is essential that you understand is that whether this life turns out to be amazing or a huge disappointment is completely up to nobody but *you*!

So I challenge you to not take the easy route through this life. Make the choices that will allow you to live the life that you truly want and deserve. Challenge yourself. Embrace the notion of living a life that truly matters. Your Heavenly Father has an amazing life full of meaning and purpose in store for you, but the choice is up to you. I implore you, make the choice to truly live your life and leave a positive impact on others that will last for generations to come. And when the time comes for you to leave this earth, you can look back and say to yourself, "Wow, what a ride!"

The time is now. Speak to your Lord out loud with a voice of conviction and say, "Heavenly Father, I'm ready to make the change!"

I implore you to stop living in utter frustration and unhappiness and create the life that you are capable of. If you truly desire to live a life of happiness and fulfillment, you must take the initial step and *make the choice*.

Develop Unwavering Faith

"This is where your peace of mind is found."

Faith: *The* Essential Component

When observing the world around you, does it seem as though the world is growing more dangerous by the day? Many feel as though global affairs are becoming more volatile as time goes on. A quick look at the daily news would reveal turmoil and conflict in virtually every corner of the globe. Stress levels are at an all-time high. Innovations such as the Internet, cell phones, and high-speed travel have increased the pace at which the world moves. The combination of these things oftentimes leave us shaking our heads in disbelief and creates a sense of uncertainty about what the future may hold.

When viewing the current state of affairs, it may leave you wondering how a person is to stay calm, confident, and happy when society continues to deteriorate and seems to be heading toward darkness and negativity.

If you are truly sincere in your search for a life without worry, with lower stress levels, with peace of mind, as well as fulfillment and true happiness, then it is absolutely essential that you develop a foundation of unwavering faith in your life.

The Origins of *Your* Faith

Have you ever stopped and taken a moment to think about the origins of your faith or perhaps the reason for your lack thereof? I'm willing to bet that the majority of people reading this book—and most people in the world, for that matter—have never stopped to consider the notion of how they came to develop their faith or belief system. Many have never sincerely asked themselves the question, "Why is it that I believe what I believe?"

The truth of the matter is that consciously or unconsciously, the majority of people in this world believe what they believe about religion, politics, and life in general because of what they have been told by others.

Now you may ask, "By 'others,' to whom are you referring?"

By "others," I am simply referring to anyone outside of yourself. It could be your parents, teachers, friends, or maybe even other sources such as corporations or the media.

English author Edward Bulwer-Lytton once famously stated, "The pen is mightier than the sword," in regard to the power of the media in persuading public opinion.

I'm not trying to reprimand you or make you feel guilty. I'm simply trying to bring awareness to the notion that a large number of the beliefs that most people hold about life are not beliefs of their own creation.

Are *You* in Control of Your Own Level of Happiness?

I want you to take a moment and ask yourself this question of logic. If the beliefs that you hold about the world in which you live are not of your own creation, then how are you expected to be in control of your own life and ultimately your own level of happiness? The answer is that if you have or are receiving a significant amount of your beliefs about life from someone other than yourself, then you are not in control of your life or your level of happiness.

It is for this reason that I encourage you to get a fresh start and reevaluate your belief system for yourself. I'm challenging you to wipe the slate clean and apply this line of questioning to every and all aspects of your life. I'm challenging you to become an independent thinker.

Don't be afraid to ask yourself the tough questions. Ask yourself, "Why it is that I believe what I believe?" and really consider if those beliefs truly make sense and align with what you genuinely feel in your heart.

Take Your Own Journey

The one area that you should begin with this line of questioning is in regard to your faith. The chances are, just like most people, myself included for a number of years, your beliefs and ideas about spirituality and faith were passed down and inherited from your parents.

Don't mistake what I'm getting at here. I'm certainly not suggesting that everything that you've been told your entire life by those who raised you is wrong or not true. I'm simply asking you to examine these issues for yourself and draw your own conclusions.

As a matter of fact, my beliefs today regarding faith closely align with those that were taught to me by my well-intentioned elders as a boy. The only difference is that the beliefs that I hold today are my own rather than those given to me by someone else.

And after all, let's face it, when we are young, our brains are not capable of analyzing complex concepts such as politics and faith. When I was a kid, I couldn't even decide who my favorite football team should be, so when I asked my father who his favorite football team was, and he said that it was the Pittsburg Steelers, it was then decided I too would become a Steelers fan.

It was much the same way with numerous other opinions that I received from my father growing up, from my favorite color to my favorite type of hot-rod. Truth be told, like most boys, I wanted nothing more than to be like my dad when I was a kid.

I'm still a big Steelers fan to this day, and my favorite color is still blue, not because it was my dad's but because now I've decided for myself that I really like it.

But when it comes to something as complex and significant as our faith and spirituality, it simply is not good enough to accept and attain your beliefs by default.

If you truly desire to be happy for the rest of your life, it is imperative that you establish your spiritual beliefs for yourself and be sure that it is truly what you believe in your heart, not simply something that you've blindly accepted because that's what you've been told your entire life. It is important for you to realize that faith is a key component that is absolutely necessary for you to develop in order for you to attain the life of your dreams and to be truly happy.

So How Do I Determine What I Believe?

I do realize that when faced with these "deep" or "complicated" questions concerning faith and spirituality, many people tend to feel intimidated or overwhelmed. The result is that most people either just go ahead and continue to listen to what they are told by others, or they simply avoid the subject of spirituality altogether. The problem with this way of thinking is that you can never achieve a life of true happiness unless you find deeper meaning in life.

God Is Most Certainly *Not* Dead

The well-known phrase referenced above originates with the renowned German philosopher Friedrich Nietzsche. In his writings, Nietzsche spoke of the future of mankind and its progress. Nietzsche believed that man would eventually evolve into what was called an "uberman" or superman. This uberman would become so sophisticated and intelligent there would simply no longer be a need for the Christian God. After all, man would become fully capable and self-sufficient, so there would no longer be a viable role for God in the lives of these immensely intelligent and capable human beings.

I believe that in today's society, due to our vast advancements and innovations in the field of technology, many have become extremely prideful and egotistical. As Nietzsche had predicted, many feel as though there is no longer a need for God in our advanced, high-tech world. We've become blinded by our own accomplishments. We live in abundance and luxury. We've become "fat and happy," as the saying goes. Unfortunately, most people are not happy.

It is no secret that throughout history, mankind has been quick to turn from God. In the Old Testament, even the Israelites felt as though they no longer needed God shortly after he delivered them from the hands of the Egyptians. It didn't take long for them to begin to complain about their situation, and some even suggested returning to Egypt and resuming their lives as slaves. After all, slavery certainly wasn't the life that they wanted, but it would sure beat dying in the middle of the desert. And then came the ultimate insult, when the

Israelites made and began to worship the golden calf. It is surprising how quickly the Israelites had lost their faith and had forgotten what God had done for them in allowing them to escape to freedom, even going as far as parting the Red Sea in the process.

Other examples can be found in the book of Judges, when the Israelites time and again turn and conducted "evil in the eyes of the Lord" despite being delivered from the grips of their enemies repeatedly by the Lord (Judg. 6:1, NIV) Numerous examples can be found throughout the Bible of people showing a lack of faith and turning from God after he had blessed them.

How is it, one may ask, that after performing a multitude of miracles and answering the prayers of a nation, they could forget so easily and quickly what their God had done for them? And yet here we are today, a nation full of abundance and comfort, founded on the virtues and ideals of our loving God, living among His blessings every day, and yet many have abandoned their faith and have allowed our arrogance to blind us to the fact that we wouldn't be here today without the blessings of our Heavenly Father.

The United States' history is full of examples of God's divine hand guiding us toward our destiny. Let's face it, the fact that thirteen small colonies defeated the most powerful military in the world is a miracle in itself.

The list of the miraculous events that have shaped this great nation goes on and on, and once again, men have become so prideful as to think that they no longer need God in their lives.

But with the turmoil and strife facing society today, it is imperative for our very survival that we do not turn our backs on the One Who got us to where we are today. Now is the time, more than ever, that we should offer our gratitude and pray that our Heavenly Father lead us through these troubled times.

I remember a discussion that was held once in the classroom. The class was discussing Middle Eastern culture. We were reviewing the practice of daily prayer and the role of religion throughout the Middle East. I inquired to my students as to why they felt that religion and its role was so embedded in Middle Eastern society while here in the United States, religion continues to take a lesser role in society as time progresses.

One student in particular offered a great answer to this question. He made the point that perhaps it is because the Middle East is full of violence and turmoil, which leads to more people leaning on God for strength. I was taken aback by the analytical response from such a young man, but upon hearing it, it triggered an internal dialogue within me that I would carry on for the rest of the day.

My conclusion was that I believe that what the student had to say contained a great deal of truth. In the United States, we have become so accustomed to the abundant, relatively peaceful lifestyle that we've come to know and enjoy that we no longer feel as though we need God in our lives. The truth of the matter is that we have become so accustomed to the amazing blessings and favor that God rains down upon us each day that we have begun to take them for granted.

But despite the relative safety that we enjoy in our daily lives, the truth remains that by allowing our Heavenly Father to take a backseat to the multitudes of other endeavors in our lives, we have created a society that has become lost, full of hopelessness and depression.

Answer His Call

It doesn't matter if you've never had any exposure to the church, religion, or even to God because you too are being called to Him. In ancient times, one only knew God when they were told of Him by others. In the book of Jeremiah, God states that under the New Covenant, "I will put my law in their minds and write it on their hearts. I will be their God, and they will be my people. No longer will a man teach his neighbor, or a man his brother, saying, 'Know the Lord,' because they will all know me, from the least of them to the greatest," declares the Lord. "For I will forgive their wickedness and will remember their sins no more" (Jeremiah 31:33–34 NIV).

Whether you have known God prior in your life or not, He has written His name on your heart, and He desires to have a relationship with you. In order to attain the happiness and fulfillment in your life that you desire, you must answer His call.

Humble Yourself

Another example of arrogance and an inflated ego is the feeling that one can accomplish everything that they set out to do on their own. It's important for us to realize that in order for us to gain and hold on to happiness, we must acknowledge that we cannot do it alone. What I mean by this is that despite the fact that we may be capable of achieving a certain level of success and happiness through our own actions, if we neglect to acknowledge the fact that we may need assistance from our Heavenly Father, He will make it evident and humble us eventually.

We must realize that in order to attain and maintain an amazing life, we must lean on our Heavenly Father in both good times and bad. Whether it be to seek guidance or to overcome challenges that may arise, our Lord wants us to be aware of the fact that He is ever present in our lives and that not only is He willing to step in and help us achieve happiness, but He wants nothing more than to give us the life that we truly wish to live!

Through a Child's Eyes

When we are children, we see the world through naive, innocent eyes, where anything is possible. Our world consists of characters such as Santa Claus, the Easter Bunny, and the Tooth Fairy. When we are told stories of these characters, there's no doubt in our young minds of their existence. When we woke up on Christmas morning, there was no doubt who delivered our presents. Or when we found a dollar under our pillow where there had been a tooth, we were filled with excitement, thinking to ourselves, "The Tooth Fairy does it again!"

If your childhood was like mine, it also consisted of biblical characters as well, such as Adam, Abraham, Moses, and Jesus. Although these biblical figures were and are real, it's sometimes hard to differentiate in our young minds between fictional characters that are for fun and real-life figures that we learn about in history class and in church.

When we asked Santa for all the gifts that we wished to receive on Christmas, there was no doubt that he would do his best to deliver. The same could be said when we prayed to God at night. When we are young, there is not a speck of doubt in our hearts when it comes to our belief and faith.

The problem lies then in the fact that as we grow older and begin to realize that many of the characters we are told about as children in good-natured fun are not real, we in turn become cynical and doubtful in other areas of our life as well.

Our attitude becomes negative at times, and we find ourselves saying things such as, "Well, that could never happen to me" or "that would never work out in my life."

Therefore it is of vital importance that we regain that unwavering faith that we once possessed as children in terms of our faith in God. It's time to begin believing again wholeheartedly that God can and is at work in our lives each and every day. If we fail to do this, we will never truly be happy.

In the book of Matthew, Jesus told His disciples that "unless you change and become like little children, you will never enter the kingdom of heaven." (Matthew 18:3 NIV) I believe that what Jesus was saying was that we need to remember the purity in which we believed in God when we were children, without an ounce of doubt in our hearts or our minds. We need to find and recapture the sheer integrity of faith that we possessed when we were young. Only then can we be happy and live the type of life that God truly desires for us.

Worry Dissolved

According to the American Institute of Stress, stress levels in the United States are at an all-time high. As a matter of fact, high levels of stress can be attributed to a variety of major health issues, including high blood pressure, increased risk of heart attack and stroke, excessive eating (which leads to a number of issues in itself), along with a myriad of other ailments. The institute states that 44 percent of Americans feel more stressed today than they did five years ago and that three out of four doctors' visits are for stress-related ailments (www.stress.org/stress-is-killing-you/).

Throughout the Bible, Jesus discusses the importance of trusting in God and having and maintaining your faith regardless of your situation. Prior to establishing my faith in God, I always felt stressed, anxious, and worried about life. Like millions of others, my focus was always on what could or would go wrong with whatever endeavor I was pursuing at the time.

The good news is that when you establish an unwavering faith in God, no matter what types of challenges you may face as you go through life, you can be certain that God is in control and that things will work out according to His plan.

Do you see how amazing this is? What a relief! This takes all the worry and anxiety out of your life. If you truly believe in God and trust that He is always looking out for your best interest, then there will never be anything to worry about.

In the New Testament, Jesus frequently speaks of having unwavering faith. One of the most famous stories of the Bible, and one of my favorites, can be found in the book of Matthew. It tells the story of Jesus walking on water.

If you recall, it was at night, and the disciples were on a boat in the Sea of Galilee. They saw something illuminated in the dark and moving toward them. Initially they were frightened, thinking that it was a ghost. But as Jesus got closer, He called out, "Take courage! It is I, don't be afraid" (Matt. 14:27, NIV).

Interestingly enough, the part of the story that is oftentimes overlooked is that at the moment that the men realize that it is Jesus, the disciple Peter became so overwhelmed with joy that without hesitation, he jumped out of the boat and started running toward Him.

It wasn't until he became aware of the fact that he too was walking on water that his logical mind took over. Realizing the sheer impossibility of what he was doing, he became afraid and almost fell into the sea, but before he went under, Jesus grabbed him and saved him.

It was at this time that Jesus spoke the famous words, "You of little faith, why did you doubt?" (Matt. 14:31, NIV) I remember hearing this story as a child and again as a young man, but I had never fully grasped what had truly transpired.

What I realized as my faith deepened is that this story illustrated far more than what it seemed. Although it was miraculous and amazing that Jesus had just walked on water, the message that He was trying to convey to His disciples was that if your faith is strong enough, there is nothing that *you* cannot do, even when it comes to walking on water!

Unfortunately for most of us, our faith is weak. We want to believe, but our minds and hearts are full of doubt and skepticism.

Oftentimes when our faith is tested, we become like Peter. Peter was capable of the unthinkable when he saw Jesus and acted out of pure faith, but then disbelief and logic kicked in, and he realized how absurd it was that he thought that he could walk on water as well. As soon as a single ounce of doubt crept in, what he was actually doing suddenly became impossible in his mind.

This very same situation occurs in the lives of millions daily. We may find ourselves working toward a goal, and things are going exactly according to plan, or we're in a relationship, and it's going better than we could have ever imagined, and then suddenly doubt creeps in. We begin to expect something to go wrong. We think to ourselves, "This simply can't be going this well, something's got to give." And then it does.

But if we were to simply maintain our faith and not allow the doubt to creep in and sabotage our minds, things would work out according to plan. But just like Peter, we oftentimes allow our minds to get the better of us.

One of my favorite verses in the Scripture in regard to faith is Matthew 7:7, in which Jesus states, "If you have faith as a grain of mustard seed, you can say to this mountain, be moved from this place to that, and it will be moved, and nothing will be impossible to you."

Jesus was telling His disciples a message that would reverberate throughout time, that if we simply believe and have faith in our Heavenly Father, we can literally move mountains! Jesus was stating that nothing is impossible for us in this life if we develop unwavering faith.

Control What *You* Can

Wrestling can be a tremendously challenging sport both physically and mentally. It is somewhat unique in the fact that it is not very often that we see men physically locked in grueling one-on-one combat. Due to the enormous pressure of competing on a stage where it is only you and your opponent in front of crowds that can get as large as forty-two thousand fans (Iowa set the record in 2015), it is absolutely essential for an athlete to have control of their emotions and display an extreme amount of poise.

As an athlete, I can remember my emotions being all over the place at times before a big match. I remember my palms feeling clammy and my heart rate going through the roof. As I grew older and matured as an athlete, I began to seek out and read more literature regarding sports psychology and the mental game and came to the realization that there were ways to alleviate the stress and anxiety that would inevitably arise before a meet.

The tools that I would learn and then apply allowed me to significantly decrease the level of anxiety that I would feel before competing and allow me to feel more relaxed before going out on the mat. The end result was an improved mind-set and better performance.

In turn, I was able to convey some of the knowledge that I had acquired throughout my career to my athletes when I began coaching. One of the most valuable lessons that I had passed on to my athletes was that they should only focus on the aspects of competing in which they were in control.

Examples of elements of a match that an athlete can control are their level of conditioning before entering competition, the moves that they would try to execute during the match, and their mind-set and focus before, during, and after competing.

Aspects of the match that they could not control included the level of their opponents' conditioning, the moves and countermoves that their opponent would attempt throughout the match, and various calls made by the referee, both good and bad.

It is absolutely essential in order to minimize stress and anxiety before and during the match that an athlete focus only on the things that they can control and let go of the things that they cannot.

This lesson applies not only to wrestling but to virtually every other sport as well. In football, a team has control over their preparation before game day, the plays that they will call, and how well they will execute those plays.

However, they do not have control over elements such as the weather, the plays executed by their opponents, and again the referees.

This is an invaluable lesson that can be carried over into each and every one of our lives. We must accept the importance of proper preparation in regard to whatever goal in life that we are pursuing and focus only on the things that we can control and let go of the things that we cannot.

For example, we have complete control over how much work, as well as the quality of the work, we put toward achieving our goals. We also have control over our mind-set, remaining positive and optimistic while pursuing our life's work.

It is no secret, however, that there will be times when certain aspects of life will simply be out of our control. It is precisely at these times that we should lean on our faith and trust in our Heavenly Father to allow things to unfold according to His divine will. After all, everything that occurs in this world is the Father's will, both good and bad.

So Why Is the World Filled with So Many Nonbelievers?

Unfortunately, as mentioned earlier, it is no secret that God seems to be taking on a smaller role in modern society. I believe there to be a number of reasons that some today lack faith. First, I believe that the questions that spirituality poses are too daunting for many people—questions such as, "Why do bad things happen to good people" or "How do we know that God is real?"

Admittedly these questions are very complex and most, if not all, do not have simple answers. I certainly am not one to claim that I have all the questions of the universe figured out, but we cannot allow the fear of these overwhelming questions and the stress that may be associated with trying to find the answers keep us from having a relationship with our Creator.

Secondly, I believe that in today's world, many people refuse to accept ideas or beliefs without a substantial amount of empirical data. We live in a world full of numbers and statistics. Every news outlet is full of political polls and scientific studies that inundate us with information, percentages, and survey results.

The reason for this is because when we attach a statistic or some sort of data to whatever the topic of discussion, it suddenly becomes more believable. Human beings feel as though if there is a statistic attached to information, then the information, in turn, becomes more concrete. It becomes something that can be proven. If there is not a statistic or number attached to the subject, many people become skeptical.

And yet other nonbelievers are turned off of the topics of faith and spirituality due to the negative connotation that is oftentimes associated with organized religion. Truth be told, wars and conflicts have been fought for centuries, and millions have died in the name of religion. Sometimes it even seems as though those who consider themselves to be the most devout can also be the most judgmental.

But when it comes to conflict and people passing judgment on others, I offer the fact that those who conduct these practices are breaking some of the most fundamental teachings of Christ. After all, Christ preached a message of peace and love, stating that you should love your neighbor as yourself, that you should not judge lest you be judged yourself, and that you should forgive men when they sin against you, and your Heavenly Father will also forgive you.

Miracles Are All Around Us

The truth of the matter is that if one were to look, they would find evidence of God's existence all around. Many people feel as though miracles are a thing of the past, but nothing could be further from the truth. Miracles are ever present in our lives every day. The Bible is full of stories of the miracles of God, witnessed by the multitudes in the past. The parting of the Red Sea, Daniel in the lion's den, and Jesus turning water into wine are well-known stories throughout the world. People tend to pose the question, "If God is real, then why do we no longer witness His miracles?"

My response to that question is that we are living in God's miracles each and every day. I remember taking an earth science class during my freshman year in college. While learning about the orbits of the planets, the earth's gravitational pull, and all the mind-blowing facts about the universe, a startling thought came to mind. I recall thinking to myself, "This is proof that there is a God!" How else could the amazing laws of science be explained? How else could all these things work in such harmony?

As a matter of fact, many scholars today agree that the odds that human life could emerge here on earth on its own accord are miniscule. The fact that precise conditions needed to occur at precisely the right time completely by happenstance in order for life to exist on Earth is highly improbable. Rather, there had to have been some sort of Creator or Intelligent Design involved (http://www.reasons.org/articles/probability-for-life-on-earth).

I'm always astounded when I hear the ongoing debate between scientists and theologians about whether or not God exists. I feel as though science and religion compliment and support one another immensely.

I am certain that when looking back on the events of my life, I can see God's divine hand at work. I have realized that many of the twists and turns that have occurred throughout my life have been far too coincidental to simply have happened by chance.

I also believe that if most people were to take a serious look at their own life and were honest with themselves, they too would be able to find instances in which everything fell into place and things ended up working in their favor when it seemed as though the opposite was bound to occur. This was not by chance, but rather due to the workings of our Heavenly Father.

The problem is that so many of us take so many things for granted. Oftentimes we do not fully appreciate the multitude of blessings that we live with each and every day. Blessings such as our health are not fully appreciated until we suffer illness. But in reality, there are so many things that can go wrong with our health that every day that we are not sick is truly a blessing.

Of course, we could always find aspects of our lives that could be better, but we can also always find areas in which things could be worse, and we are very fortunate and should be extremely grateful for what we have. We are truly living in God's divine blessings every day.

Miracles Are Impossible *without* Faith

If you are not receiving the things that you would like out of this life, there's a chance that your faith is not at the level that it needs to be. The New Testament is full of accounts of the miraculous acts performed by Jesus during His time here on earth. Time and again, Jesus speaks of the importance of one's faith in order for miracles to occur.

The book of Matthew tells the story of a demon-possessed boy. Initially, Jesus's disciples tried to heal the boy, but with no success. After the failed attempt, the boy was brought to Jesus, and He rebuked the demon, and the boy was healed.

Afterward, the disciples inquired to Jesus as to why they were unable to drive out the demon. He replied, "Because you have so little faith" (Matthew 17:20 NIV).

The book of Mark tells of a woman who had suffered from a bleeding disorder for twelve years. Despite receiving treatment from doctors, her condition grew worse. The Bible states,

> *"When she heard about Jesus, she came up behind Him in the crowd and touched His cloak, because she thought, 'If I just touch His clothes, I will be healed.' Immediately her bleeding stopped, and she felt in her body that she was freed from her suffering.*
>
> *At once Jesus realized that power had gone out from him. He turned around in the crowed and asked, 'Who touched my clothes?'*
>
> *'You see the people crowding against you,' his disciples answered, 'and yet you can ask, 'Who touched me?'*
>
> *But Jesus kept looking around to see who had done it. Then the woman, knowing what had happened to her, came and fell at His feet and, trembling with fear, told Him the whole truth. He said to her, "Daughter, your faith has healed you. Go in peace and be freed from your suffering"' (Mark 5:27–34, NIV).*

Do you see the significance of this statement? Jesus didn't say, "*I have healed you.*" Rather he said, "*Your faith has healed you.*"

The same chapter tells a story of the daughter of one of the synagogue rulers named Jairus. While Jesus was healing the woman with the blood disorder, some men came to inform Jairus of the unfortunate news that it was too late, his daughter had already passed away.

Ignoring what they said, Jesus told the synagogue ruler, "Don't be afraid. *Just believe.*" Jesus and a few disciples went to Jairus's house to see the girl. He then emptied the room except for his disciples and the girl's parents. Jesus then spoke, "Little girl, get up!" (Mark 5:41) The girl got up and was healed.

Why do you think that it was important for Jesus to clear the room of everyone except for those few people? Jesus knew that He could not afford to have doubters in the room because the miracle may not have come to fruition.

Numerous stories can be found in which Jesus speaks of the absolute necessity of faith in regard to performing miracles. If your faith is strong enough, I promise you will begin to see God's miraculous work take shape in your life.

Faith Makes the Impossible, Possible

In the book of Hebrews, the apostle Paul speaks in great length about the importance of maintaining one's faith. Paul cites the multitude of examples in which faith allowed miraculous acts beyond all human comprehension to occur. Paul states that faith "is being sure of what we hope for and certain of what we do not see."

He goes on to elaborate on the role of faith in our world, discussing examples such as, I paraphrase, that by faith the universe was formed, Noah warned about things not yet seen and, in holy fear, built an ark. He says that "Abraham went to a place he had not seen, and made his home in a promised land, for he was looking forward to the city with foundations, whose architect and builder is God. Even though he was past age, Sarah herself was barren, was enabled to become a father." Paul points out that from Abraham came descendants "as numerous as the stars in the sky and as countless as the sand on the seashore."

He goes on to say that through faith, Moses's parents hid him for three months after he was born because they saw that he was no ordinary child, that Moses refused to be known as the son of Pharaoh's daughter, and that he sprinkled the blood so that the destroyer of the firstborn would not touch the firstborn of Israel. Moses passed through the Red Sea on dry land.

Paul also points out that faith allowed the walls of Jericho to fall and the patriarchs of the Bible to conquer kingdoms, administer justice, and gain what was promised. Faith shut the mouths of lions, quenched the fury of the flames, allowed men to escape the edge of the sword, allowed weakness to be turned into strength, allowed men to become powerful in battle, and raised the dead to life.

We must realize that we serve the same God that produced the miracles of the Bible that we have become so familiar with. We must also realize that those same types of impossibilities are still possible today, but only if our faith is strong.

Faith will play a vital role in your life. Faith will show you a way when there is no way. Faith will find a cure when there is no cure. It will give you hope, when there is no hope. It will allow you to endure when all seems lost. It will open doors when all seem shut. It will change your life in ways that simply are not fathomable to the human mind. And it will make the impossible possible.

Just as He did with the matriarchs and patriarchs of the Bible, God wants to display His power to the world by performing miraculous works in our lives, but first we must establish unwavering faith!

Strengthen Your Spiritual Muscle

Unfortunately, I cannot tell you how to attain unwavering faith instantaneously. We are not robots or machines, in which with the flip of a switch, our faith can be turned on at full throttle. Rather faith can and has to be attained by continual, persistent exercise and effort.

Just as if you would like to build strength in the muscles of your body, faith must be conditioned and strengthened through time and experience. Nobody goes into the gym and bench-presses three hundred pounds on the first day. It takes weeks, months, and sometimes even years to attain such a tremendous level of physical strength. But those who are dedicated, disciplined, and determined enough will eventually find themselves performing that very feat.

The same goes for developing one's faith. Initially when seeking our Heavenly Father, we may find ourselves struggling in the area of faith. But through a daily exercise regimen of faith-building exercises, you will begin to notice a gradual increase in your spiritual muscle.

When I speak of faith-building exercises, I am referring to a number of things. It could be dedicating ten minutes per day to reading Scripture or devoting yourself to prayer both morning and night. Other examples would include reading a faith-based book, or even just challenging yourself to ask and find answers to the tough questions regarding your spirituality.

Standing up to, facing, and overcoming challenges will also strengthen your faith. Trusting in the Lord, even when things seem grim, only to come out better off than before, allows us to confirm in our hearts that God is in control.

One of my favorite scriptures is found in James 1:2, which states, "Consider it pure joy, whenever you face trials of many kinds, because you know that the testing of your faith develops perseverance."

Wax On, Wax Off

Growing up, one of my favorite movies was *The Karate Kid.* If you're unfamiliar with the movie, it entails a teenage boy named Daniel LaRusso, who has moved to a new town. Things seem to be going well until the boy meets a love interest who just so happens to have an ex-boyfriend who, along with his friends, uses their skills in martial arts to bully the young man.

Long story short, an elderly karate expert takes Daniel under his tutelage and teaches him the way of martial arts, allowing him to defend himself, and by the end of the movie, he wins the county karate championship and, of course, gets the girl.

The reason that I'm mentioning this movie is that throughout the film, the karate master uses a very interesting and unique training method. You see, after Daniel and the master agree that they will become student and teacher, the elderly man begins subjecting the boy to seemingly pointless manual labor. Daniel paints the fence, sands the deck, and waxes the old man's cars. Daniel tends to think that these chores are payment in exchange for the training that is to occur in the future.

But in reality, the master has been training Daniel the entire time through the use of the various tasks of manual labor. Finally, when Daniel has had enough and confronts his sensei about all the meaningless work that he has been subjected to, the master begins an onslaught of strikes directed at his pupil. At this time, the student reacts with muscle memory created through the monotonous motions of painting, sanding, and waxing. He realizes that his wise old master was training him all along in the martial arts, albeit without him knowing it.

My point is that just as the old master was training his pupil in *The Karate Kid*, your Heavenly Father is developing the skills in you that you will need in life, also sometimes without your knowing.

Have you ever wondered to yourself, "Why is this happening to me?" or maybe "Why do things never go my way?" or even "Why can't I have an easier life like others that I know?" When you find yourself in these situations, asking these types of questions, it is imperative to remember that you are being shaped and developed into the person that you *need* to be so that you can go forth and fulfill your purpose on this earth.

For it is in these times of hardship and struggle that the Lord in heaven is teaching you the necessary skills for life.

Peace of Mind at Last

When you have strong faith in God and deep spiritual convictions, you can stop worrying about every aspect of your life. Most people go through life from day to day completely stressed out, always expecting the worst. I once asked a class full of students, "When you attempt to do something, do you expect the best and that things will work out, or do you expect the worst?"

I was somewhat disappointed, but not completely surprised, when most of the class replied that they usually expected the worst. When I dug a bit deeper and questioned as to why that was the case, the general response was that they always worried and expected the worst so that if things didn't work out the way that they had hoped, they wouldn't be disappointed.

This conversation made me realize that this is probably how most people approach their chosen endeavors. The problem with this approach is that worrying and expecting the worst could possibly be the reason that one does not accomplish a particular goal. Not to mention this way of thinking leads to excess stress, anxiety, and even health problems such as ulcers and high blood pressure.

Jesus Himself told His followers not to worry, for our Heavenly Father would always provide for us. He said in Luke 12:24 (NIV), "Consider the ravens: They do not sow or reap, they have no storeroom or barn; yet God feeds them. And how much more valuable you are than birds!" This is such an exciting notion because this means that God is always in control; therefore, we can live worry-free.

An Amazing Display of Faith and Forgiveness

On the morning of October 2, 2006, tragedy struck a small Amish community in Lancaster Country, Pennsylvania. After the children had returned from recess, a would-be shooter walked into the school. He allowed the adults and boys to leave but took ten young girls hostage. Eventually the man shot ten of the girls, resulting in five deaths, before turning the gun on himself, subsequently ending his life.

The horrific story made headlines across the country and left many in complete shock and disbelief. The nation was left shaking its head with a number of unanswered questions such as, "What would drive a man to murder innocent children in cold blood," "Why do such horrific things happen," and "How can this community heal from such a tragic loss?"

Despite experiencing one of the most tragic events imaginable, the Amish community reacted in a way that would display some of the deepest convictions of faith and forgiveness.

Rather than allowing themselves to resort to rage and feelings of revenge, the Amish community leaned hard on their faith. Their leaders urged them to remember the shooter's family and offered prayers to give them strength.

The Amish elders then went on to not only pay a visit to the family of the shooter, but some even attended the man's funeral. According to an article by pennlive.com, one of the community leaders led a prayer, stating, *"I pray for this man's wife and the load she must be carrying. Father, help her deal with this in the hard days ahead. Let us find peace."*

I remember hearing about this powerful story of the forgiveness that was demonstrated on that day and the profound impact that it had on me. I remember thinking to myself, "This is the epitome of the forgiveness that Jesus had encouraged for us all during his time here on earth."

I remember thinking upon hearing the story that justice must be served and that there must be a reckoning for what this man had done! But upon hearing the stories of forgiveness, I felt an immediate shift in my perspective.

The Amish leaders didn't question God for allowing such a heinous crime to occur. Nor did they seek revenge against the killer. Rather they stayed true to their faith and overcame the evil with good just as the scripture speaks in the book of Romans.

The reaction of the Amish community not only allowed the anger to dissolve, but it also allowed the healing to begin.

As it has been said, it's not whether or not you will face adversity in your life but rather when. I encourage you that regardless of the trials that you face in life, stay strong in your faith. Know in your heart that no matter what happens, it is the Father's will. We simply cannot understand all the happenings of this earth. At times, bad things will happen to good people and vice versa, but we have to stay strong in our faith just as the Amish community did during their time of great tragedy.

Also, be quick to offer forgiveness. Remember the example of forgiveness that was put on display in Lancaster, Pennsylvania, in 2006. Forgive those who have wronged you in life. Once you are able to forgive, the healing process can begin. Your Heavenly Father will be proud of you for your ability to forgive. For as Jesus said in Matthew 6:14, "For if you forgive other people who sin against you, your Heavenly Father will also forgive you."

You Don't Always Have to Figure Everything Out

Problems are a part of life regardless of age, wealth, sex, or ethnicity. The good news is that you can stop worrying and overstressing about every challenge that arises. I'm not suggesting that you just simply sit back in your La-Z-Boy and put your feet up, hoping that everything will work out according to plan. You still have to do your part and make every effort possible to overcome problems and challenges, as well as to achieve your goals. But once you have done all that you can do, then it's time to sit back and let your Heavenly Father do the rest.

The author of Proverbs told us to "trust in the Lord with all of your heart and lean not on your own understanding." This means that you don't have to figure everything out. Our human minds simply just are not capable of solving every problem or challenge that we face in life, and that is fine.

Our Heavenly Father does not expect us to be able to resolve and sort out every circumstance, but He *does* expect us to have faith in Him so that He can do it for us. That is why it is imperative that we develop a deep-seated faith and a conviction in our belief that our Heavenly Father is always in control.

Developing an unwavering, uncompromising faith in God allows you to establish a strong foundation that will sustain you through anything that life may throw your way. Whether it's dealing with a personal hardship or trying to conquer a goal, by trusting and having faith in God, you will have the inner strength and fortitude to persevere.

No matter how stressful your life or how unsettling global events may become, nothing will be able to rob you of your happiness if you follow through on step 2 and *develop unwavering faith.*

STEP 3

Love Untethered

"This is where your self-worth is found."

The Most Dangerous Crisis

If I were to ask you what you feel is the greatest threat facing mankind today, what would be your response? Would it be terrorism, widespread famine, or perhaps global economic collapse? Despite those issues being valid life-threatening concerns, as a species, I feel that human beings are facing an even more dangerous crisis today. This crisis is all-encompassing and if not resolved, could mean the demise of life on earth as we know it.

This terrible problem does not deal with the economy, it is not the increase of drug and alcohol abuse, and it is not the rising tide of crime or poverty. Rather, I believe that the most daunting problem facing us today has an effect on each and every individual on this earth from every corner of the globe.

The problem that I'm referring to is a severe deficiency in love. I sincerely believe that the root of all the problems in society, including those listed above, can be traced back to a widespread lack of love. The truth of the matter is that unfortunately in today's society, most people do not feel loved, are not fully expressing their love toward others, and are certainly not receiving the love they truly deserve in their lives.

The Most Essential Need

As a species, we all share the same universal emotions, needs, and desires. The renowned educational philosopher and one of the forefathers of modern psychology, John Dewey, claimed that one of the most prominent needs for every human being on earth is that each one of us wants and needs to feel as though we matter. Everyone wants to be somebody. Everyone wants to be noticed. And it is because of this desire to matter that many of us do the things that we do in life. Think about it for a minute. It's why we play sports, act in plays, drive nice cars, and try to stay up on the latest fashion trends.

So the question then becomes, why is it so important for all humans to feel as though they matter? I think that in order to answer this question, we have to delve a bit deeper into what every human being needs or desires for his or her life. I firmly believe that the need to matter stems from an even deeper fundamental need, which is to be happy.

As mentioned in the introduction of this book, I believe that if you were to ask most people what they desired most in life, they wouldn't say money or even power, but rather they would say that they possessed a great desire to be happy. Again, the way that people believe that happiness is obtained differs from individual to individual, but the end result is the same. Some believe that happiness is found in being successful, accumulating riches, or spending time with friends and family, but ultimately all these things have the same outcome, and that is that they are attempts at finding happiness.

At the Very Core of Our Being

Although I feel that all people ultimately want to be happy, I also firmly believe that if we were to search our souls even deeper, at the very core of our being, even beyond the desire to matter or to be happy lies the most fundamental need of all. It is the need to be loved.

The need to be loved lies at the very core of every human being on earth, whether they know it or not. Regardless of where we believe that our feeling of significance or happiness is found, it all begins with the desire to genuinely feel loved. In turn, it is impossible to feel happy, significant, or important in the absence of feeling loved.

That's right, love is the foundation of all happiness. As a matter of fact, it is the origin of all other positive emotions. If one does not truly feel loved, it is impossible to attain a genuine feeling of happiness, no matter how much money or success one may accumulate or experience.

The sad truth is that many people in the world today do not truly feel loved, and as a result, many are desperately seeking to find ways to attain that feeling. People will go to great lengths to feel loved. Time and time again, people subject themselves to various types of suffering and hardships in their desperate attempt to feel loved.

Some suffer and endure through abusive relationships in their desperation to find love. Some search for the feeling of love through a dog, cat, or some other pet. Many get married in a hopeful attempt to feel loved, and some will have children, hoping to fill the void of the missing love that they've been craving their entire life.

Please do not misinterpret what I'm saying, love between two people—between spouses, between a parent and child—or even an owner and a pet is very real and can fulfill us to a certain extent, but these are all examples of what is called earthly love. We can love our children, spouses, and pets tremendously as much as is humanly possible.

But what I'm saying is that because we, as human beings, are flawed and are limited in our capabilities regarding all aspects of life, then our love and ability to love are flawed and limited as well. I wholeheartedly believe that love between two people can exist on this earth and that that love is completely sincere. But nonetheless, the love that we are capable of feeling is limited simply because we are limited. I'm confident that none of us can honestly say that our abilities, whether it be intellectual or emotional, are infinite, so therefore we must admit that we are limited simply because we are human.

But it is essential for us to understand that there exists a love that is on a level that you or I can never comprehend. It is infinite, ever present, perfect, and eternal, and it is waiting for you to accept it right now as you are reading this. It is the only love that can fill the craving that every human being feels deep at their very core. The love that I speak of is the divine love of our Creator, your Heavenly Father.

Open Your Heart

I sincerely ask that you please read the following passage very carefully. I cannot express the importance of your understanding of this next statement enough. It can and will literally transform your entire life. Take as much time as you need. Read it more than once. Read it, digest it, process it, and allow it to take root in your very soul. This statement alone will give you a whole new sense of purpose, confidence, fulfillment, and happiness that will last for the rest of your life. It reads:

"Your Heavenly Father, the Creator of the Universe, loves you more than you could ever understand or comprehend. His love is ever-present, unconditional, and eternal. No matter who you are, what you have or haven't done, regardless of race, ethnicity, sex, or monetary value, He knows your name. He loves you and is proud of you, and it will be so for eternity."

Again, I encourage you to read this statement as many times as you need in order for it to take hold of your heart. For the facts that are stated in this passage are what every human being craves in their heart to hear and know, and yet unfortunately so many are simply unaware that it is so. This statement holds true for you and everyone else on earth right now. You do not need to change or "fix" anything about yourself. The only thing that one needs to do in order to receive this love is open their heart and accept it.

After you have embraced and firmly believe what is said in that statement, your life will be transformed. You will gain an entirely new sense of empowerment, self-worth, confidence, and overall happiness in your life. You will then find that you will have the confidence and ability to not only pursue but also attain any goal in life that you may desire!

You see, our Heavenly Father loves us all on a level that is beyond human comprehension. It is incomparable to anything that we have ever experienced. The reason for this is because our human minds are limited in our ability to comprehend the extent of our Father's capabilities and also the extent of His love. And that's okay.

As mentioned in the previous chapter, God understands that our knowledge and understanding are limited, but His love is unconditional and ever present nonetheless. Although it is impossible to comprehend the extent of our Heavenly Father's love, once you have opened your heart, you will undoubtedly be able to feel it.

The only thing that one needs to do in order to receive God's love is to become aware that it exists and then simply open their heart and accept it. This is the greatest gift that one could ever receive.

The reality is that until we consciously and gratefully receive God's love, we are left with an unfillable void in our hearts and souls. Despite being brought up in church and hearing over and over again about God's love for us, I had never quite fully grasped this concept. As a result, I never truly opened my heart and accepted His love. And like many others, as I grew older, this desperate longing to fill that void in my heart continued to grow.

Like many, I became frustrated, uncertain as to why the feeling that something was missing would not go away, and at the same time, I was becoming more and more angry, hopeless, depressed, and sad. No matter what I tried, the feeling persisted. I tried everything— food, alcohol, relationships, television, and buying things—but no matter what I tried, each endeavor led to more frustration. You see, knowing of the Lord and having a personal relationship with the Lord are two completely different things.

It wasn't until I decided to make a change in my life and clean up my habits that I felt a shift. I had been praying every morning and night and had made it a point to read a few pages in my Bible each day. And suddenly one day, like a lightbulb turning on, I had an epiphany. It happened one day when I was running on the treadmill and was allowing my mind to drift. I was asking myself the question, "What does God really want out of my life?" And then I heard a quiet voice on the inside.

It said to me, "William, do you know that you are loved more than you can possibly fathom, more than you can understand, or even conceive?"

I realized that God loved me. God truly loved me. God loved me infinitely, unconditionally, eternally, and perfectly. For some reason, that had never clicked to me consciously or spiritually. You see, it wasn't necessarily something to understand. Understanding just makes us aware. It was something to be felt. This realization was life changing.

A New Kind of Love

This love didn't come from another person on earth, not even from an extremely important individual, like a president or even a king. This love came from the Creator of the universe, the heavens, and the earth, and all who inhabit it. This was a pure, never-ending love beyond all imagination.

Once I came to this realization, everything began to change. Suddenly I felt a calm like I had never experienced before. All my life up to this point, I had desperately been seeking the approval, and ultimately the love, of those around me while the greatest love in existence was always there waiting for me to accept it.

Once I had accepted His love, I then realized that I could, in turn, love myself. I began to develop a continually growing sense of self-worth and confidence, not a false facade of confidence or bravado that I had tried to portray when I was younger but a genuine feeling of worth that I had never had before. And when you realize and accept God's love for you, you will experience the very same feeling. Once you've attained a feeling of unconditional, divine love, you will then be able to go forward in life and accomplish all your dreams.

The Search Is Over

Most people go through life searching. Some aren't sure what they're searching for, and others are unaware that they are even searching at all. But the reality is that we are all searching for a sense of identity, worth, importance, happiness, and, most of all love.

The great news is that in order to obtain all these things and more, you need only to open your heart to your Heavenly Father and accept the love that He is waiting to give to you for eternity.

The truth is that our Heavenly Father has unconditional, infinite, perfect love for all of us. The problem is that some of us feel undeserving of His love. Perhaps you feel undeserving of this love for one reason or another. Many think, "There's no way God could love me. I've done so much wrong in my life. My life has been full of sin."

But to our Heavenly Father, this doesn't matter. Your age, sex, ethnicity, prior wrongs, and mistakes are irrelevant to our Heavenly Father. Make no mistake, I'm not suggesting that our God doesn't care if we've sinned or are living the wrong way right now. What I'm saying is that just like any good and loving parent, our Heavenly Father is willing to overlook our flaws, shortcomings, and mistakes and forgive us. That is why in the New Testament, Jesus continually referred to our Creator as the Heavenly Father. And just like any good parent, our Heavenly Father loves us unconditionally in spite of our flaws.

Our Heavenly Father knows that we are flawed, and because of that, we will in turn sin. He does not expect us to be perfect. In John 3:16, the Bible states that this is precisely why He sent His son, Jesus Christ, into the world to serve as an example for us to follow and then to sacrifice Himself in order to cleanse us of our sins. But before we can be cleansed of our sins, we must accept Christ as our Lord and Savior.

The only thing that our Heavenly Father asks in return is that we love and serve Him. Jesus himself, when asked what the most important of all the commandments was, stated, "To love the Lord your God with all of your heart and with all of your soul and with all of your mind" (Matt. 22:36–40, NIV).

Find Your Value

Many people go through life feeling undeserving or unloved. At some point in their life, someone, whether it was a family member or boyfriend/girlfriend, made them feel unworthy or inadequate.

Perhaps this has happened to you? Someone in your life criticized you or pointed out all your "flaws." Regardless of the motivation behind the criticism, it begins to wear away at our self-worth. It happens to us all. We all carry around some sort of emotional wounds or scars from events and experiences in the past.

It is because of these emotional wounds that people allow themselves to be subjected to physical or emotional abuse, sometimes for the rest of their lives. After one has suffered damage to their self-worth, they oftentimes feel almost as if they are not deserving of better treatment, or maybe they feel unworthy of being happy or loved.

After realizing that your Heavenly Father, the most powerful entity in the entire universe, loves you more than your human mind can possibly comprehend, you will feel and know in your heart that you deserve nothing but the best. You will develop an all-new sense of self-worth and confidence that will allow you to stand up for yourself. You will no longer put up with insults or with being mistreated by others. All those emotional wounds and insecurities will heal because you will take a whole new perspective on life and gain a new healthy self-appreciation.

Now *You* Are Capable of Loving Others

I've oftentimes heard it said that "you cannot truly love someone else until you love yourself." Although I believe this to be a completely true statement, the problem lies in the fact that oftentimes individuals struggle with the idea of loving themselves because they feel undeserving even of their own love.

The answer to this problem lies then in opening one's heart to the divine love of our Heavenly Father. As mentioned previously, this love is unconditional, everlasting, and eternal. You see, God's love is the source in which all other love flows. When God's love flows into and through you, it can then flow out to others. Once you accept God's love, you're then capable of loving yourself, and only then will you truly attain the ability to love others.

As mentioned before, that is the root of all the problems with many relationships today. Many people are looking to fill the void within themselves because they haven't opened their hearts to God. They, in turn, become frustrated and resentful toward their partner because even though they are in a relationship, the void still remains, and they're not sure why. They, in turn, blame their spouse or significant other for failing to fill that void.

Individuals oftentimes do not have a healthy love for themselves, which leads to low self-esteem. This, in turn, allows them to be either mistreated by others or, even worse, to mistreating those that they love. You will not be able to find a truly fulfilling, loving relationship until you open your heart and accept God's love and, in turn, gain a healthy sense of love for yourself.

After you've accomplished these two things, which take virtually no effort, you can then truly offer your love to someone else, as well as receive their love in return.

Connect with Your Soul Mate

I too went through a number of frustrating relationships over the years. Like most, I yearned for companionship. My weekends were a series of going out to bars and clubs, getting thoroughly inebriated, and finally getting the nerve talk to a few girls and maybe even getting a phone number.

I had been in a couple of two- and three-year relationships, each filled with a feeling of frustration and a sense that something was missing. I began to wonder if human beings were really supposed to spend their lives with only one person or if there was anyone in which we could be compatible enough with to share our entire lives. "Maybe I'm just meant to be single," I thought. And then I experienced something amazing.

As mentioned earlier, after my realization of God's unconditional love, I had gained a newfound sense of self-worth. Along with this sense of self-worth, I had also attained a new kind of confidence that I had never experienced before. This was not the false confidence that I had tried to portray for many years before in order to cover up the emotional wounds and insecurities that I had been carrying my whole life, but rather a true quiet confidence that came from knowing that the Creator of the world knew my name and loved me infinitely regardless of what anyone else said or thought. Along with this feeling came the notion that I was deserving of the best and that I shouldn't settle until I felt that I had met someone with whom I felt truly compatible.

I had bought a house in the mountains and had been spending a lot of time alone, which to some may seem very sad, but for me, I was enjoying the solitude as well as the peace and quiet. This had really given me a chance to think about some of the deepest questions of life. I truly felt that my spiritual side was experiencing tremendous growth and that my relationship with God was being nourished.

I had also been doing a lot of reading during this time. It wasn't until I was reading a book by Viktor Frankl entitled *Man's Search for Meaning* that I had an epiphany in regard to love and companionship.

Man's Search for Meaning is an amazing book about Frankl's experience in a World War II concentration camp, but more importantly, it is about his mind-set and how it allowed him to persevere and ultimately survive. One aspect of Frankl's survival that gave him the inspiration to continue on was the thought of seeing his wife again.

Even though enduring the most horrific conditions imaginable, Frankl (1946, 50) refers to the memories of his wife and how they brought joy to his heart, despite being subjected to tremendous suffering. His experience made me realize that the greatest gift that God has bestowed upon us is the ability to experience and share our love. And by not finding my soul mate and the person that I was meant to spend the rest of my life with, I was insulting God by not accepting and sharing that gift.

This was the very reason that God gave Adam Eve. He wanted Adam to experience the pleasure of sharing his love with another. I truly believe that when we are in a state of love is when we are the closest to the Divine.

So for the first time in my life, I prayed to God to bring me my soul mate. I asked God to bless me and bring me someone that I could love with my whole heart, someone with whom I was completely compatible, someone who would make my heart race, someone who could make me smile even when they weren't around. someone who would not only be my lover but also my best friend. I told the Lord that I would do my part in meeting this person by being sociable but not forcing the issue. I also let the Lord know that I would be patient in allowing this happen. I placed my trust in Him.

After the prayer, I felt a sense of calm. I knew that being with the right person for the rest of my life was something that I wanted, something that I deserved, and something that I was ready for. I was secure in the fact that my Heavenly Father loved me, and as it says in the book of Romans, "And we know that in all things God works for the good of those who love Him, who have been called according to His purpose." (Romans 8:28, NIV)

A few weeks and months passed, and I was still single, but living with a newfound sense of peace and security. I kept reminding myself that the Heavenly Father was at work in my life and that if I was patient and trusted in Him, I would be rewarded.

And then one day, unexpectedly it happened. I was chaperoning a field trip to a leadership conference. We were sharing a bus with a group of middle school students, and it just so happened that there was a substitute advisor who had filled in for the actual advisor who, by chance it seemed, had other obligations that day.

She was beautiful, so much so that I was taken aback upon first seeing her. We struck up a casual conversation and realized that we had a lot in common. We were both former athletes and still loved to exercise and live a healthy lifestyle. But the true sign came that we both realized our shared love for dogs, specifically Boston terriers.

I once had a friend tell me, "When you meet *the* one, you'll know it." At the time, I thought it was just something that people said in order to make single people feel better about being single. But after meeting my future wife, I realized that there was a great deal of truth to that statement. I had never experienced that feeling before, nor will I ever again, but it was great!

The rest is history. After a year of dating, we were married, and she and I continue to grow closer together each day.

The point that I'm trying to make is that God was waiting for me to make the spiritual changes that were necessary in order for me to have the ability to be a part of a fulfilling, healthy relationship. Prior to making the spiritual changes necessary, this healthy relationship would not have been possible.

It wasn't until I embraced His love that I had, in turn, gained a healthy love for myself and was then truly ready and capable of loving someone else.

I believe that if you too open your heart to your Heavenly Father and embrace His love, you will experience a newfound sense of self-worth and see tremendous improvement in virtually all your relationships—with your spouse, children, family, and even complete strangers.

We're All in This Together

When you take a deeper look at everyone in the United States, and even on earth for that matter, our lives are all interconnected. It's quite fascinating really, to think that we are all living our lives separately as individuals, each one with our own unique experiences, and yet we are all going through this experience called life together. Therefore, the actions of others have an impact on us, and our actions inevitably have an impact on the lives of others.

I'll give you an example. Have you ever gone into a store in a perfectly good mood, not at all feeling any negativity. Then while checking out, the cashier treats you in an unprovoked, rude manner. The next thing you know, you feel perturbed and walk out of the store in a completely different mood than when you went in. Due to your negative interaction, you may then unknowingly go on to take out your frustration on your children, spouse, or some other innocent bystander.

Or maybe you were at work and were feeling fine when a coworker says something negative or rude that completely ruins your emotional state and changes your mind-set for the remainder of the day. Suddenly, your mood went from good to bad in a matter of minutes. I think it's safe to say we've all been there.

Our Impact on Others

Some cultures refer to this notion as karma. Others call it the golden rule. Regardless of the label that you want to attach to this philosophy, the truth still remains, and the result is the same. Our words and our actions have a ripple effect on others and on society as a whole. It is important for us to remember that as we go through life, we need to make others feel the same way that we would like to feel. When you treat someone with respect, it will be reciprocated. When you say a polite word like *please* or *thank you,* it will most times be returned. And when you offer a compliment or a generous tip, you may have just made that person's day. In turn, they will go on throughout their day and likely pass that very same positivity onto their children, spouse, or maybe even another stranger.

It is our responsibility as human beings to remain mindful that everyone is dealing with some sort of challenge. For some, it may be relationship issues; for others, it could be an ill loved one, or maybe they're just overwhelmed by life. Therefore, do whatever you can, no matter how small the gesture, to ensure that you are spreading kindness and positivity.

Love Untethered

It's time for you to accept the Divine love that is waiting for you. Open your heart to the love of your Heavenly Father and find your sense of self-worth. By doing this, His divine love can then flow through you to the rest of the world. You can never be truly happy unless you implement step 3 into your life and *love untethered.*

Welcome Change

"This is where your enthusiasm is found."

The Most Terrifying Word in the Dictionary

What would you say if I were to ask you to name the most frightening word in the dictionary? Would it be *terrorism*? Or perhaps *bankruptcy*? The answer may vary from person to person, but for many, that word would simply be *change*.

Change, the very mentioning of the word can strike fear in the bravest of souls, perhaps even yours. Changes in even the simplest of endeavors such as one's route to work or morning routine can wreak havoc on a person's psyche. But what if I were to tell you that initiating and welcoming change will be one of the most beneficial steps that you will take toward creating a happy life?

After all, let's look at the facts. The very purpose for you picking up this book was because you desired to make a positive change in your life.

The problem lies in the fact that many people today do not want to and are not willing to change. But the truth of the matter is that we should all be willing to change, for if we possess the desire

90

to improve and to attain lifelong happiness, we must be willing to change, *for it is impossible to improve without change.*

When change occurs, one of two things inevitably occurs. The first is that our situation gets worse. The second is that it our situation gets better. But have no fear, for in your case, when change occurs, the conditions of your life are guaranteed to improve, and things are destined to get better due to the acquisition of the knowledge laid out before you in the pages of this book and your dedication and continual effort to implement this knowledge.

It is important to let go of the negative connotation attached to change if we are ever to create the amazing life that God has in store for us.

Why Fear Change?

In order for us to welcome change, we must first understand why so many people are reluctant to do so. The reason for this is actually relatively simple. You see, it is human nature to do everything in our power to avoid stress and stressful situations. Many people associate stress with pain, discomfort, and possibly even death.

Therefore, human beings are always striving to find a place in our lives in which we feel safe and comfortable. As a matter of fact, we refer to this place as our "comfort zone." But failure to step out of one's comfort zone could quite possibly be the most detrimental mistake that an individual could ever make in their entire life.

People like to be in their comfort zones because when we're in our comfort zone, we feel safe. We know what to expect and therefore will not be forced to deal with an unknown or unexpected circumstance that could result in pain, perhaps in the form of stress. Stepping out of your comfort zone means stepping away from things that may be familiar and, in turn, forcing you to face the unknown.

But if we are sincere about creating a happy life, then it is absolutely necessary that we accept a certain degree of stress in our lives in order to initiate change and growth.

Growing Stronger

A good comparison of enduring stress in order to gain strength is in regard to strength training in order to grow stronger physically. For example, if you desire to gain an increase in strength or muscle mass, you will need to place a substantial amount of stress on the muscle in which you desire to strengthen. This is because of the fact that each time that you pick up a weight that is almost too heavy for you to lift, it actually places stress on the muscle to the point that it creates tiny microtears within the muscle.

When you leave the gym and go home and rest after the workout, your body begins to repair the damaged muscle. The muscle in turn grows and gets stronger in order to adapt to the stress that was placed upon it.

Despite the fact that lifting weights and stressing the muscle can be extremely uncomfortable at times, it is imperative to do so if a person desires to gain strength.

A person could spend hours in the gym, but if the individual only lifts a weight that is comfortable and is lifted with little to no effort, the muscle will not be stressed sufficiently and therefore will not adapt and grow. Placing stress on the muscle is absolutely essential in order for it to grow stronger.

Similar to stressing one's muscles, stepping out of one's comfort zone can at times be very stressful and uncomfortable. But if you truly desire to grow mentally, spiritually, and emotionally, then you have no other choice but to force yourself to step out of your comfort zone.

Please do not forget that an essential component in order for your body to repair the damaged muscle is that you must also provide the proper nutrients. Protein and essential amino acids are necessary for muscle repair and growth.

The nutrients that allow for us to adapt, change, and grow mentally, emotionally, and spiritually are found in our mind-set. By providing the proper mental/spiritual nutrition through our focus and attitude, our spiritual and mental strength will grow.

The key to initiating and following through on change is to be aware that it may be uncomfortable, but still keep a positive perspective on what you are trying to attain by making this change. If you are not able to maintain the right perspective on why it is that you are trying to make this change, it is likely that your mind-set could veer toward the negative, causing you to resent the entire process. This could lead to ultimately abandoning your attempt, leaving you trapped and frustrated in the same situation that you've been trying to leave behind.

The Number 1 Enemy of Growth—Comfort

As I've already mentioned, most human beings will do just about anything to avoid feeling uncomfortable. But what we must realize is that ironically enough, the only way for us to experience personal growth is to make ourselves uncomfortable.

Throughout my teaching career, I would oftentimes deal with parental intervention when it came to various aspects of the educational process. As a matter of fact, an aspect of education that is continually becoming more frequent is the number of legal requirements placed upon educators regarding educational modifications, plans, and accommodations customized for individual students.

What I mean by this is that parents will take legal measures in order to address various issues with their child regarding anything from extensions on homework assignments to allowing their child an unlimited amount of absences, to even allowing disruptive behavior within the classroom. One parent in particular went as far as contacting all her child's teachers and guidance counselor in order to ensure that her daughter would not be required to speak in front of the class.

I realize that all these requests were made out of genuine love for one's child. No parent wants to see their child receive a failing grade or be subjected to the utter fear that some feel when speaking in front of the class. But at the end of the day, by offering a way out of these stressful situations, the parents were actually taking away from their children the opportunity to grow and develop as human beings.

School teaches young people a tremendous amount about what to expect in life, as well as offers an opportunity to develop a number of essential life skills. Lessons such as being on time, personal accountability, responsibility for one's actions, and social skills that are vital to possess in the world today are all acquired through the educational process.

So when a parent takes measures in order ensure that their child is excused from various assignments and even school itself, they are hindering their child's development because they are avoiding the very actions that will mold their child into a productive human being.

Many of us in life have tried and continue to try to avoid discomfort in a very similar fashion. Nobody likes to be put in a situation that is considered uncomfortable, but the truth of the matter is that that could be the very thing that is keeping many from becoming the very best that they could possibly be.

Speaking from personal experience, and I believe that most people would agree, the times that I have experienced the greatest personal growth throughout my life is when I was faced with and overcame the greatest adversity.

In Order to Grow, You Must Give

Another reason that people may avoid change is because they are afraid of what they may be forced to give up. Perhaps someone who is trying to get into great shape physically would fear that they would be forced to give up their favorite food. Someone who is trying to start a business may fear that they will be forced to put in long hours and have to deal with a great deal of work-related stress and time away from home.

Many people avoid walking with God due to the fact that they view the notion of living righteously as boring and possibly uneventful. They do not want to give up all the things that many consider to be fun. A lifestyle of partying and alcohol consumption and the things that go along with that type of lifestyle can sometimes seem more appealing to some but will always eventually result in a life of emptiness and utter sadness.

Lastly, there is oftentimes a fear of success. Many might think that this sounds ridiculous, but believe it or not, fear of success holds a tremendous amount of people back from pursuing and attaining their goals and dreams. This, in turn, prevents them from ever truly being happy.

The fear of success is very real. Some feel as though the attainment of success would usher in a new standard that would be expected by others to be upheld and maintained. One may feel as though they would not have the ability to maintain this new standard, which could ultimately lead to failure, as well as a feeling of disappointment from themselves and those that they love. This, in turn, could lead to as a loss of self-worth. These are all irrational thoughts and fears, but for many they are very real.

It is extremely important that you do not allow fear to hold you back from pursuing and attaining the changes that are imperative in your life in order for you to acquire and maintain lifelong happiness.

Overcome Fear with Bold Convictions

A notion that may be comforting to know is that it is okay to feel fear at times. An important fact to consider is that fear is nothing more than misdirected emotion and energy.

Although it may seem somewhat counterintuitive, fear can serve as a positive force in your life. I say this due to the fact that fear can actually be a very powerful motivator. But it is important not to allow fear to grow, fester, and turn into a negative force. Allowing this to happen can be toxic. It is extremely important that instead of allowing fear to have a negative effect on your psyche, you transform it into positive motivation.

Imagine yourself not accomplishing the change that you are pursuing and then using that to motivate you to take action. Ask yourself, "Do I want to be stuck in this situation forever?" Or even better, "Do I really want to live out my years unhappy, frustrated with myself for not pursuing my life's dreams, ultimately living my life unhappy?" The obvious answer is a resounding no! Therefore, you must move forward boldly and courageously. This is where the development of the strong foundation built upon your faith and the love that your Heavenly Father has for you is absolutely essential.

An amazing example of the type of conviction that is necessary for you to succeed in life can be found in the well-known biblical story of David and Goliath. When the prophet Samuel came in search of the "man after God's own heart," he identified possibly the least likely candidate, the shepherd boy who was the youngest and perceived weakest of Jesse's sons.

But as the story goes, despite the doubts of others, Samuel identified David as God's chosen one. David had been going back and forth between tending his father's herd and bringing his brothers food on the battlefront where the Israelites were locked in a standoff with the Philistines.

One day while David was bringing his brothers their food and preparing to report back to his father in order to assure him of their well-being, a Philistine giant came forward and issued a challenge to the Israelite warriors as he had done every morning and evening for forty days. Upon hearing the insults hurled toward the Israelites, mocking their God, David was overcome with rage.

The other soldiers looked at one another with fear, no one brave enough to step forward to face the giant, but David was appalled that the men were allowing these insults to go unpunished, so he resolved to do something about it.

In the book of 1 Samuel, the Bible states that David went to King Saul and said, "Let no one lose heart on account of this Philistine; your servant will go and fight him" (1 Samuel 17:32 NIV).

David grabbed his sling and headed off to the battlefront with the deepest conviction, knowing that there was nothing to fear because his God would protect him and guide his hand in battle.

Before we move on with the story, we must first consider David's faith and examine how he was able to develop such a deep-seated conviction. You see, David was looked down upon by his brothers and the other men as a pesky boy. What they didn't know is that his faith had been developing and strengthening for years. Imagine the many nights that David spent alone, tending his flock of sheep. Imagine the beautiful expanse of the moonlit sky and stars that David stared upon night after night in wonder and awe at the Lord's divine splendor. In his mind, I'm sure that this scene helped solidify that only a being of Infinite Intelligence could possibly create such a magnificent universe.

God knew the conviction that David held in his heart. That is precisely why he sent the prophet Samuel to call upon him, because He knew that this type of faith and conviction would be absolutely necessary to overcome the giant in order to demonstrate God's power and to later rule as king over God's chosen people. And although

David seemed like the least likely candidate to conquer the brute, the book of Samuel states that the Lord reaffirmed that David was the chosen one when He said, "The Lord does not look at the things people look at. People look at the outward appearance, but the Lord looks at the heart" (1 Samuel 16:7 NIV).

I oftentimes think of what that scene must've been like that day on the field of battle. The standoff had been going on for weeks. Each day, the Philistine giant would come forth and issue a challenge to the Israelites. He would challenge any man from Israel who thought that they stood a chance, then laugh and mock them as they all looked at one another and shook their heads with fear and disbelief at the sheer size and audacity that the monster possessed.

It had to seem humorous then to the men when word spread around camp that the young shepherd boy from the fields had volunteered to stand up to this great warrior.

I'm sure that the majority scoffed, laughed, and ridiculed the boy about the inevitable outcome. Perhaps the giant would cut off his head immediately or maybe toy with him a bit, like a cat with a mouse?

I'm sure most agreed, "This is not going to turn out well for our side." They probably even felt pity for such a young man to be sent to the slaughter.

King Saul tried to give David his armor and weapons, probably thinking to himself, "I'll give this kid some credit. At least he's trying to step up when no one else is willing to even make an attempt."

But David told Saul that he didn't need the armor. After all, he had never worn armor before, and it could only hinder his performance. In the past, all that he needed to kill encroaching lions and bear was his trusty sling.

King Saul must have been surprised and possibly even felt a tinge of guilt for sending the boy to his death. He had to be thinking to himself that this was a suicide mission.

I've seen depictions of this event captured on film. Oftentimes David is portrayed approaching Goliath timidly, creeping forward, step by step with a look of apprehensiveness.

But this is not how I see the encounter play out in my mind. I envision this scene much differently. In my mind, I see David approaching his adversary with a confident stride, looking forward to the opportunity to prove the strength and power of his God. Eventually, unable to restrain himself, David's stride turns into a sprint, stopping only once he was within striking distance of his enemy.

Standing on the battlefield, Goliath had to be thinking that it must have been some kind of joke when he saw the shepherd boy standing across from him.

I believe that David had not an ounce of fear in his heart. He had not a speck of doubt. He didn't see all the what-if scenarios in his mind. Rather, he felt a combination of the deep-seated conviction that his Heavenly Father's love would guide his hand and a burning anger inside at the very thought of this "uncircumcised Philistine" having the audacity to stand against the Israelites and, more importantly, against their God! He knew in his heart that God was with him, and therefore, he had nothing to fear.

He courageously declared to the Philistine, "All those gathered here will know that it is not by sword or spear that the Lord saves; for the battle is the Lord's, and He will give all of you into our hands" (1 Samuel 17:47 NIV).

As the story goes, David dropped the giant with a direct hit to the forehead with a single shot from his sling. Without a second of hesitation, he ran forward and stood over the monster, grabbed the Philistine's own sword, cut off his head, and held it high for all to see.

You can only imagine the hush that fell over the armies of both sides as they stood in disbelief, thinking to themselves, "Did that just happen?" A few seconds later, when reality had set in, the Israelites let out a war cry, charged, overtook their enemy, and seized the day.

The events that followed in David's life are well known. His victory that day set the stage for his ascent to the throne, and it would be within his very bloodline that Jesus Christ would later be born.

Although this story has been told for centuries, I believe that the moral of the story is oftentimes overlooked. The title "David vs. Goliath" has been used to describe a multitude of modern-day competitions and events from NCAA Basketball to the Little League World Series. Normally when this label is applied, it refers to an underdog taking on a much stronger opponent.

But there's a greater lesson to be learned from the story. I believe that when looking at David vs. Goliath from an analytical perspective, the meaning runs much deeper than just an underdog overcoming the odds on favorite.

What we need to realize about the story isn't necessarily *what* happened (David wins), but rather *why* David, the perceivably weaker underdog, was able to defeat Goliath, the perceivably much-stronger adversary.

It is important to take note of the fact that this confrontation and David's victory took place in order to display the importance of the role that faith plays in one's life and also to demonstrate God's power and divine will.

Think for a minute about the fact that David was a shepherd before earning fame and admiration far and wide. Being the youngest of Jesse's eight sons, he was given the lowly job of watching over and taking care of his father's herd. Do you think that David enjoyed this job? The most likely answer would be no. David probably would have rather been on the battlefield with his older brothers, which would have been seen as a far more respectful endeavor than tending sheep.

But serving as a shepherd boy allowed David the opportunity to develop and strengthen his faith. Imagine, night after night, David trying to protect his father's sheep from predatory animals. He most certainly said more than a few prayers to his Lord in heaven, asking for protection and guidance in staving off would-be threats. Each night that David emerged victorious, his faith grew stronger. By continuing to face and overcome challenging situations David was able to develop immense faith that later allowed him to fulfill his divine purpose.

Not only did David's faith grow as his Heavenly Father continued to protect him and keep him safe night after night, but tending and protecting the flock also offered him the invaluable opportunity to develop his skills with the sling.

I believe it safe to say that David, by watching over the herd and continually being exposed to and able to overcome challenges day after day, night after night, was able to develop the faith and the aim that would one day lead him to not only victory on the battlefield but also to his divine destiny. Had God spared David from the lowly act of serving as a shepherd, in turn taking away his opportunity to overcome challenges, David most likely would never have defeated the Philistine giant on the field of battle that day and, ultimately, would never have ascended to the throne of Israel.

What you need to realize about this story is that you too should carry the same type of conviction that David displayed on the battlefield that day in your very own heart, for you too serve the very same God that allowed David to conquer courageously on the battlefield and overcome insurmountable odds, and He is willing to do the same for you.

There's a good chance that throughout the years of hardship and struggle that, just like David, God has been preparing you to become the type of person that you need to be in order for you to persevere and fulfill your potential. Stop looking at challenges as something negative in your life and look at them as an opportunity to grow and improve.

When fear and doubt try to bombard your mind, you need to force them out and realize that the God that gave David the strength to overcome a giant is the same God that loves and watches over you as His own.

Guard Your Mind

Unfortunately, when you reveal your life's ambitions to others, there's a good possibility that you too, like David, will face the ridicule of naysayers. It's a fact that there may be times when others, due to a feeling of envy, may try to sabotage your success. It is precisely at these times that you must maintain your deep conviction, because just like David, you too will have the favor and love of your Almighty Father to sustain you through the greatest of challenges. You simply cannot afford to allow others to derail you from achieving your dreams and desires.

Goals: Your Road Map to Happiness and Success

If you are truly sincere in making permanent changes of a positive nature in your life and achieving lifelong happiness, it is absolutely necessary for you to set meaningful goals.

Many of you may be wondering, what is the purpose of setting goals? The answer is simple. A goal is like a magnet that pulls you forward toward your better self. It serves as a destination on your road map of life. It gives your life direction. Without goals in life, you will be like a ship lost at sea, floating aimlessly in the sea of life without a purpose or destination.

One major problem for many who wish that their life would change is that they've been stuck in the same routine and with the same habits for so long, they're not even sure how to initiate the changes that they desire.

The process for initiating and creating change in your life is fairly simple. Notice that I've used the word *simple*. I certainly did not say *easy*. There's a major difference between the two.

For example, if a person would like to set out to change their health, they would need to focus on changing their eating habits, as well as implementing an exercise routine.

These two areas of one's life can be relatively simple but will require a great deal of discipline, willpower, and resolve in order to become successful.

The first step to take in developing your goals is to identify the specific areas that you wish to change. Then take a step back and give this area in your life some thought. Ask yourself what exactly will need to take place in order for you to make the changes that you want to achieve?

You should then write two to three of the goals that you've created on an index card. You should then carry that card in your pocket with you at all times as a constant reminder of what it is that you've set out to accomplish. You should read this note card aloud at least twice a day, once in the morning upon awaking and once in the evening before you go to bed. This certainly doesn't mean that you cannot read it as many times as you wish throughout the day.

Be sure to be specific. For example, do not simply write, "I will become healthier." Instead you should write, "I will lose ten pounds in six months."

Another example of an overly generalized goal would be, "I will become more financially secure." Instead you should write, "I will have $5,000 in my bank account by the end of the year."

An area in which continuous personal growth is imperative if you are to ever be happy is in your spiritual life. Some meaningful goals towards improving the quality of your spiritual life may be to take at least ten minutes per day to read and study Scripture or perhaps to pray or meditate both morning and night each day.

One Swing at a Time

As a young boy, I went through a phase of having the urge to cut down trees with an ax. I'm not exactly sure why, but I believe it had something to do with watching a movie about the tall tale of Paul Bunion. Regardless of the reasoning, I wanted to cut down trees. The interesting thing is that I would unknowingly learn a valuable lesson about the pursuit of goals while swinging that ax.

My grandfather was kind enough to oblige and pointed out a few trees that were in need of being cut down. As I was wielding the ax and chopping away at the tree, swing by swing, I felt my heart rate climb and sweat begin to run down my forehead. I was overcome by a feeling of determination and excitement. But as the tree fell, something else began to happen, something that I didn't even realize. With each swing of the ax, as wood chip after wood chip fell to the ground, I could see progress being made. It felt good to see progress being made with each swing. I could see my effort paying off.

Looking back, I now realize that while chopping down those trees in the forest behind my grandfather's house, I began to experience the pure joy of working hard toward a goal and then experiencing a sense of accomplishment when finished.

The tree had become my goal, and I actually found myself embracing the hard work that went into chopping down the tree. I cut down two or three before my grandfather had no more trees that needed to be cut down, and I felt satisfied, my thirst to swing the ax quenched.

But looking back today, I now realize that I learned a valuable lesson when cutting down those trees at my grandfather's house. I learned that when we are pursuing goals, we oftentimes get into a hurry. We set our minds upon a meaningful goal, and then we expect to achieve the goal with minimal effort or perhaps even no effort at all.

But there's a great deal to be said regarding the hard work that is put toward achieving a goal. Believe it or not, I oftentimes have found the pursuit of a particular goal to be more rewarding that actually achieving the goal itself.

Just as in taking down a tree, our goals will not be accomplished with a single swing, but rather by taking it one swing at a time while maintaining constant effort and perseverance. By staying the course and remaining diligent in your pursuit, the goal will be all the more gratifying once you succeed.

Don't Spread Yourself Too Thin

You will also want to be sure to prioritize your goals. What I mean by this is that you should only focus on two to three goals at a time. The reason for this is that because each individual has only a limited amount of resources in which to dedicate to any specific goal at any given time. What I mean by resources are time, energy, and possibly finances. Therefore, you must be careful not to spread yourself too thin, thus taking away your ability to give substantial effort toward the pursuit of any of your goals.

Although you may have a dozen goals that you wish to accomplish, if you get too overzealous and try to accomplish too much at once, you will most likely not achieve any of them. You must prioritize which are the most important goals and then pursue those goals initially. After you have achieved those particular goals, you may continue on to pursuing the others.

A good metaphor for focusing on only a few goals at a time is the act of putting out a fire. Imagine that you have been tasked with extinguishing a fire using a fire hose or extinguisher. If you were to move the hose back and forth too quickly over an area too large, you would limit the amount of water dowsing any particular area of the fire thoroughly, resulting in failure to extinguish the fire.

On the other hand, if you were to focus the hose on a particular part of the fire, it would be far more effective. Once that particular part of the fire was extinguished, you could then move on from place to place until the entire fire was completely out.

The great innovator and man most often credited with creating the first practical telephone, Alexander Graham Bell, once made this statement in regard to the importance of focus, "The sun's rays do not burn until brought to a focus."

You too should focus your energies to burn like the sun. If you allow yourself to be spread too thin, accomplishing your goals will never come to fruition.

See Your Future and It Will Be So

Another practice that you should conduct on a daily basis is visualizing the changes in which you wish to see in your life in your mind's eye. You can do this while driving your car (while maintaining your awareness of the road, of course). You can also do it while in the shower or while pumping your gas. Begin to see yourself as you are to become, and you will automatically begin to gravitate toward becoming the person that you envision yourself to be.

Develop a Deep Level of Resolve

One of the most important aspects of achieving your life's goals and ultimately attaining lifelong happiness is to develop a deep level of resolve.

Webster's Dictionary defines *resolve* as, "to make a definite or serious decision to do something." Notice that this is not just some casual decision or goal that you've decided to pursue one day in passing. This is a *definite* change that you've decided to make with a great deal of thought because you *know* that you *must* make that change in order to be happy!

Stop Allowing History to Repeat Itself

There have been a number of significant philosophers and great thinkers who have famously stated that history repeats itself. An analytical look at history would prove this statement to be entirely true. There have been numerous events, themes, and cause-effect situations that have happened time and again throughout history.

The deeper question then lies in not whether or not history repeats itself, but rather why it repeats itself. My father always used to say, "Times change, people don't."

This simple yet profound statement is very true. On a global scale, history tends to repeat itself because human nature tends to remain the same. There are always those who seek more power, territory, wealth, etc. Therefore, you see reoccurring events and themes throughout history as these human tendencies continue to play themselves out.

If one would analyze his or her own life, they would most likely find that situations and events tend to repeat themselves time and again in a similar fashion.

Perhaps an individual has difficulty maintaining employment. They bounce from job to job wondering why they keep getting let go.

Or maybe a person continues to experience failure in their relationships one after the next. If those individuals were to take a closer look at their lives, they would realize that they continue to experience these same negative situations in life because they continue to display the same undesirable behaviors.

As a matter of fact, some time ago, I came to this realization in my own life. I had been going from one frustrating relationship to another until I finally stopped and said to myself, "What am I doing wrong here?" I really had to analyze my actions and find the common theme as to why I was unable to find a fulfilling relationship. I had to see where it was that I was continually making the same mistakes.

I didn't look at myself or my relationships in a critical manner, but rather in a more analytical, problem-solving way in order to determine what I could do differently so that I could change the quality and the outcome of my relationships.

I quickly realized that I was living my life in the wrong manner. Alcohol was always a factor in creating problems. I also realized that I was continually settling for partners in which I was not completely compatible.

Once I had identified the common theme or problem, I could then take the necessary action to ensure that I no longer made the same mistakes in the future and, in turn, experienced a different outcome.

Once the changes were made, as mentioned earlier, I was able to find a partner with which I was completely compatible and happy.

Break the Cycle

Whether you realize it or not, you may be experiencing a very similar cycle of negativity in your life. There are various repetitious themes and situations continually occurring in your life because of the inherent qualities, habits, and behaviors that you continue to exhibit. Oftentimes people tend to be egotistical in their self-analysis, making excuses and placing the blame on others. For some, it can be difficult to admit their mistakes or flaws.

The good news is that we are in complete control of our decisions and therefore in changing the events that occur in our own lives. If you have a negative cycle of events occurring repeatedly throughout your life, you can stop the cycle by simply identifying the behavior and then changing it.

In order to do this, you need to take an honest look at yourself and ask yourself, "What behaviors am I continuing to display that are repeatedly leading me down this undesirable path?" Remember, no excuses or blaming others, you are the one responsible for your own life. You must hold yourself accountable.

An example would be if you have fallen into a state of being unhealthy or overweight, take responsibility and identify the problem. Perhaps you have repeatedly begun various workout programs but continue to lose interest or just plain stop shortly after beginning?

You need to take responsibility for the fact that you have not been following through on the goals that you've put into place. You also need to realize and be aware that if you do not make getting healthy a concrete goal and follow through on making it happen, you will ultimately end up disappointed, unhealthy, with an ongoing feeling of guilt and general unhappiness.

We're All Human

It's important to note that you should never be afraid to admit that certain areas in your life need work. It is only when these areas are honestly assessed that you can identify the problem, set your goals, and take the necessary actions to see those goals through.

Remember the Pain

The legendary wrestling coach Dan Gable implored his athletes to remember the pain that they felt after their losses. Please do not be confused about what I've just said. I certainly did not suggest that Dan Gable wanted his athletes to dwell on their losses. If Gable told his athletes to dwell on their losses, he definitely would not have been able to lead his Iowa Hawkeyes to twenty-one Big Ten titles and fifteen NCAA titles, including nine straight!

Rather, Dan Gable wanted his athletes to learn from their losses and then move forward, but he also wanted them to remember the bitter pain that they felt deep down inside when they lost. Gable knew the power that pain can hold over an athlete. When times got tough in practice and the wrestler wanted to gear back on his intensity or call it a day, the renowned coach wanted his athletes to draw upon the pain of their losses and use it as extra motivation.

Anyone who has competed can relate to the fact that when athletes are nearing the final phase of practice, one has a tendency to allow their mind to get the best of them. It tells them to slow down, take it easy. Focus begins to wane, the mind starts to drift, and thoughts begin to venture toward the post-practice hours when the athlete can get a nice cold drink or perhaps something good for dinner. It starts to question their purpose for being there and whether or not it's worth it. It starts to criticize the coach, "Who is he to tell me to go another round anyway?"

Dan Gable knew this tendency of the mind. He also knew how badly his top-level athletes hated to lose. That is why he wanted them to remember the disappointment, the heartfelt anguish, the frustration, and utter disdain that were present immediately following a match in which they ended up on the losing end.

And Gable knew too that it was imperative to draw strength from and utilize that very pain as motivation. He also knew that that is what would make the difference between whether that particular athlete would become a champion standing atop the podium at the end of the season or just another name on the never-ending list of "pretty goods."

From Tragedy to Triumph

You see, Dan Gable knew something about using pain as motivation to turn tragedy into triumph. As a matter of fact, Dan Gable knew a lot about it. His story is well-known throughout wrestling circles, but if you are unaware, allow me to fill you in.

Dan Gable was and is not only one of the most successful and dominant coaches in all of athletics (the best, in my personal opinion), but he was an amazingly successful wrestler in his own right. Dan Gable himself will attest to the fact that much of his success can be attributed to his own personal tragedy.

When Dan was a boy, his family experienced one of the most horrific tragedies that a family could be forced to endure. While away on a family outing, Dan's teenage sister was brutally raped and murdered in the family home. As could be understood, the family was shocked, in a state of disbelief, and uncertain of how to move past this tragedy.

But rather than dwell on the loss of his sister and allow it to tear his family apart, Dan chose to honor his sister's memory by dedicating his wrestling career to her. Dan was already a highly successful wrestler, but with the added motivation of honoring his sister, he was able to compile an undefeated record throughout his high school career.

But the story doesn't end there. Dan would go on to wrestle for one of the most storied programs in collegiate wrestling, the Iowa State Cyclones. It looked as though Dan would finish his stellar collegiate career undefeated as well, but it wasn't to be so.

As fate would have it, Dan was defeated in the *final match* of his career at the NCAA championships by a relatively unknown wrestler in a match that many felt would be an easy victory.

Once again, Gable was faced with a challenge that a lesser man would not have been able to overcome. But just as before, Gable pulled himself together and used the pain to motivate himself to go on and dominate at the next level.

Dan Gable would go on to win the gold medal in the 1972 Olympics in Munich, Germany. Not only did he win the gold, but he did not surrender a single point throughout the entire tournament (*Dan Gable: Competitor Supreme*).

And so Dan Gable carried the lessons that he had learned throughout his life into his coaching career. During his coaching career, Dan Gable became a master motivator and developed an uncanny knack for knowing exactly how to read and inspire his athletes. He used the pain of past losses to motivate his athletes, allowing him to coach his Iowa Hawkeye teams to an unheard of record of 355–21–5! By the time his coaching career came to an end, he had coached 152 All-Americans, 45 NCAA national champions, 106 Big Ten champions, and 12 Olympians, including three bronze, one silver, and four gold medalists (dangable.com)!

You Too Must Remember the Pain

And so just like a Gable-trained athlete, you too must remember the pain associated with your "losses." I know what you may be thinking, "But how can I, I've never wrestled?" Perhaps you've never even participated in competitive sports? I understand that, but what I'm referring to when I use the word *losses* is any time in your life where you've fallen short of a goal and felt emotional pain associated with a particular experience.

For example, perhaps you have allowed yourself to get to a point in your life where you've become extremely unhealthy and out of shape. As a result, you motivate yourself to get on a good diet and exercise program. After two months, you see tremendous results. What can sometimes happen to people is that the pain begins to subside. After all, you're looking pretty dang good, and so you begin to gradually slip back into your old habits.

Perhaps one day you say to yourself, "I've been hitting the gym hard six days a week. It's not going to hurt to skip one workout." Or maybe your diet has been going great so you decide to allow yourself to have a beer or soda. Little by little, you begin to skip workouts or eat junk food more frequently. Eventually, before you even realize that it's happening, you're back to your original weight and appearance, and the depression, frustration, and pain associated with how you look and feel return once again. You realize that history has just repeated itself.

There's a lot of truth to the old adage "Time heals all wounds." And because this is true, many of us fall short in the areas in which we want to change. That is precisely why it is imperative for you to remember the pain.

Again this bears repeating, I'm certainly not implying that you dwell on your mistakes or relive the past. As a matter of fact, nothing could be further from the truth. Beating yourself up and dwelling or hanging on to past mistakes will only hold you back in life. Rather, what I'm saying is that just like a Gable-trained athlete, you must draw on the emotional pain of the past for strength in times in which your motivation is waning.

When your mind begins to tell you that it's okay to skip that workout or eat that junk food, remind yourself of the pain that you felt before you were able to make positive changes in your life.

Do Not Get Sucked Back into That Unhealthy Relationship

This same notion could be applied to various areas of our lives including relationships. Oftentimes it can be very difficult to get out of an unhealthy relationship. But once out, it's of vital importance not to get pulled back in, which happens more frequently than we'd care to admit.

The reasoning for this is because as time progresses, we tend to forget the pain that was caused during the relationship. Despite the reason, whether infidelity, disrespect, or some other reason, the pain often subsides, which in turn opens the door for forgiveness, and the relationship gets rekindled, many times resulting in the same outcome as before.

It is important that when that ex-boyfriend or ex-girlfriend is texting you late at night wanting to see you, you remind yourself of the pain caused by the all the lying, cheating, and deceitful behavior that you were forced to endure while in the relationship.

You deserve better. Your self-respect and self-worth will no longer allow you to be treated that way. You will find someone better and more deserving of your love.

Welcome Change

As mentioned at the beginning of the chapter, change is something that many people cringe at the very thought of. But in reality, when we think of change, we should get excited because it is when you begin to welcome change, take action, and make positive changes in your life that you can truly begin to experience a genuine feeling of happiness.

Therefore, resist change in your life no longer. Turn your perspective on change into something positive to be looked forward to. After you begin to apply step 4 to your life and begin to *welcome change*, you will begin to experience the improvements in your life that your heart has been longing for.

STEP 5

Free Your Mind

"This is where your power is found."

Are You Brainwashed?

One day while teaching a lesson on the use of propaganda during WWII, I asked my students the simple question, "Do you think that you are brainwashed?"

Of course they looked around the room at one another with confused looks (which was a telling sign in itself), and they all began to shake their heads no.

I went on and said, "The fact that you are all unaware that you are brainwashed is even more troubling than the fact that you are."

I then followed up with, "I am brainwashed as well to a certain extent, but the difference is that I am aware of it."

Obviously I wasn't suggesting that any of my students, or myself for that matter, had ever been taken captive by nefarious forces and subjected to hours of horrific mind manipulation and torture. I was simply using the influence of modern advertising as a comparison to the propaganda that was used by both sides during the war.

But the truth of the matter is that all of us, from the time that we were infants, have been exposed to various types of conditioning that have not only inevitably affected the way that we think about and view the world but have also had an effect on our core beliefs and values. Although the term *brainwashed* may be a bit extreme, I believe that it is fair to say that we can all admit that we have at least been influenced in one way or another from time to time by the media and advertisers.

The fact of the matter is that the person that we are today is a combination of genes, experiences, and core beliefs that we have developed over time. Have you ever stopped to think about how you have come to develop your sense of fashion, your hairstyle, or even why you own the car that you drive? What about your political beliefs or, as mentioned earlier, your spiritual beliefs?

The reality of the matter is that some people have gotten a significant amount of their core beliefs from sources other than themselves.

Let's face it, we inherit most of our beliefs from our parents when we are young, and then as we grow older, our greatest influence shifts to our peer group. Most of us today are living according to the advice, as well as the influence, of others.

"Do You Like Having a Good Time? Then You Need a Good Watch!"

Has there ever been a time in your life in which you made a conscious decision based on the opinion of someone other than yourself? When it comes to my fashion as an adult, a story about my early days as a teacher comes to mind. When starting my teaching career, like most young professionals, I had little money, and this fact was evident when it came to my wardrobe.

The phrase used above was taken from one of my all-time favorite movies, the boxing classic *Rocky*. I had always gotten a good chuckle upon hearing the line, but never was this statement driven home for me as much as it was one day while at school.

Ever since college, I had been wearing an old cheap wristwatch that I had purchased for only a few bucks. The watch looked cheap and flimsy, but it had served me well throughout student teaching and my first few weeks of school after starting my new job.

The watch was functional, so buying a new one wasn't at the top of my priorities list when I had officially started my teaching career, but that was about to change.

One day while making copies in the faculty room, a colleague of mine was passing by and took notice of the cheap piece of metal on my wrist. He made his repulsion quite evident to everyone in the room when he yelled out, "What is this thing," while simultaneously grabbing my wrist and holding it up for all to see.

Most of the room was gracious enough to pay little attention to the outburst, but their thoughtfulness did little to ease the pain of the embarrassment, which was evident due to the redness of my face.

Needless to say, one of my initial purchases with my first paycheck was a respectable-looking watch.

Looking back, I could have blown the guy off. I should have said to myself, "Nobody really cares about what kind of watch I'm wearing. After all, the one I have is perfectly fine."

But I, like most people, was fearful that if I didn't go out and purchase a more expensive watch, it could result in yet another embarrassing incident.

Most people have experienced a similar or comparable situation, and looking back on the event, I realize that I began to be more mindful of my professional dress in order to keep ridicule from others at bay.

The point that I'm trying to make is that oftentimes we make our choices in life regarding our style, as well as other facets of our lives for that matter, based upon the opinions of others. Many of our decisions that we make in our everyday lives are based upon what we believe other people will think or what we have been conditioned to believe by others. And with the advent of social media, many have become almost obsessive about posting a picture or status and anxiously waiting to see the number of likes, shares, or comments that they get in response.

Virtually all people are conformists to a certain extent. After all, the level of stability enjoyed by a particular society depends upon it.

But too much conformity can be dangerous. For example, had the Nazi regime been met with more opposition, it could have prevented a tremendous amount of violence and death in the world. John F. Kennedy once stated, "Conformity is the jailer of freedom and the enemy of growth." The truth is that many people find themselves conforming to the beliefs and attitudes of the society in which they live, without any thought given as to why?

The influence that the media and corporate mass marketing can have on the culture and beliefs of a population is astounding. But conforming to social norms can not only have a negative impact on society, it can also be detrimental to an individual's pursuit of happiness.

The Trap of Conformity

In order for you to be completely happy, you must first find the courage to break away from the social norms imposed upon you by society. When it came to the issue of conformity and the importance of fitting in with others, a number of questions came to my mind, including, "Why are human beings so desperate to fit in," "Why do some feel that it is absolutely essential to be accepted by their peers," and "Why are people so quick to conform to social norms?" In order to attain true happiness, I feel as though these questions must be answered.

I've come to the conclusion that human beings are hardwired for conformity. You see, I believe that conformity is a primitive survival instinct that human beings have continued to carry within our DNA since ancient times. Thousands of years ago, when life was much more dangerous and resources were scarce, conforming in order to fit in with the herd was absolutely essential to a person's very survival. Trying to survive on one's own meant lacking the protection of the group, as well as fighting off predatory animals by oneself. It also meant the possibility of not being able to acquire enough food and resources in order to survive.

Therefore, our ancestors were driven by necessity to conform in order to fit in and be accepted by the group. In the dangerous world in which they lived, being a part of the group was literally a matter of life or death. Being rejected and forced out on your own was most likely a death sentence.

Despite technology and society evolving throughout the centuries, the human psyche still carries with it many of the same instincts that allowed us to survive in a much more dangerous ancient world. I believe that human beings have carried this survival instinct into the modern era. This leads many to feel as though conforming and fitting in is an absolute necessity.

Think of the efforts put forth by many in order to keep up on the latest fashion trends or the obsessiveness carried on by millions to continually check social media in order to stay up to date on the latest news and gossip. What about likes and Retweets? I ask you, is it really that important to attain the approval of others on social media? Why do most people care so much about whether or not they are liked by others?

From a logical standpoint, the answers to these questions simply do not make sense. It really shouldn't matter if you are up to date on the latest fashions, if you are in the loop on the latest happenings, or even if your coworkers like you or not, but for many, it simply does. Since so many people are unaware as to why they are so desperate to fit in with the crowd, they fail to break free from the social pressure to continually adhere to the behaviors of modern society.

"What does it hurt if I conform to the social norms?" you may ask. That's a completely fair question. Unfortunately, the answer isn't so simple.

I ask you to take a moment to think about this notion. If you truly desire in your heart to be happy, but the majority of people in which you are conforming with are not happy, then logic states that you too will not be happy.

Therefore, if you truly wish to attain the happiness that you desire, it is absolutely imperative that you recognize and address the extent to which you are conforming to the rest of society and break free.

Jesus, the Ultimate Nonconformist

An interesting fact that many do not realize about the message that Jesus brought to the earth is that His teachings were considered to be completely revolutionary at the time. None of the religious scholars at the time were preaching the type of message that the Messiah had delivered directly from God.

The God that was spoken of by the Pharisees and other religious scholars was a wrathful God that demanded that the Law be upheld at all costs. The religious Law of the Old Testament was to be followed to the letter, and those who did not follow it would face severe repercussions.

If Jesus truly wanted to fit in and be considered an authority on religious tenets by His peers, He too would have continued to preach the same message that the scholars of His time were teaching. There's no doubt that He would have found favor in the eyes of the Pharisees had He aligned Himself with their teachings. But Christ's purpose was to reveal *the truth*. Jesus did not conform to the message of other teachers. Rather, He taught the people of a God of love and forgiveness, a Heavenly Father or *Abba* who loved His children and desired to have a relationship with them.

Jesus's nonconformist message would continue to grow and spread throughout the world, even after His ascension into heaven. It is important for us to realize that even in today's world, conforming to societal norms is not always in our best interest. You should not be willing to conform to a world that is so full of negativity and evil. This is precisely why the book of 1 John states, "Do not love the world, nor the things in the world. If anyone loves the world, the love of the Father is not in him."

When we speak about the evils of the world, we are referring to negative elements such as materialism, violence, sexual promiscuity, and drug and alcohol abuse, among other earthly pleasures.

Therefore, if you desire to live a life in the tradition of Jesus Christ, go forth and love, forgive, do not abide by the ways of the world, and have the courage to be a nonconformist.

Stop Following the Crowd

A good example that comes to mind when speaking about the willingness and pitfalls that we may be subjected to when we follow the crowd rather than doing what is right occurred one day while in school. On this particular day, the school was conducting a fire drill.

As per protocol, each classroom had a predetermined route it was to take in order to evacuate the building in the most efficient manner possible and in order to avoid congestion in the hallways and stairwells. Despite the fact that some of the predetermined routes that the students were to take to leave the building didn't seem to make sense, the procedure was thoroughly planned and well-thought-out.

Ignoring the predetermined evacuation plan could lead to severe congestion in the hallways, and ultimately a large crowd would form. In the event of an actual fire, this could be dangerous, if not fatal.

I was on my planning period during this particular fire drill, but as I was heading toward the appropriate exit, I began to pass a number of students from another classroom heading in the wrong direction. I knew one of the students, so I pointed and said, "Your class is supposed to be using this exit."

The student looked at me and then looked at her classmates and, in a conflicted manner, replied, "This is the way everyone else is going."

I said, "I know, but everyone else is using the wrong exit, and the procedure is for you to exit using this door."

As the student weighed her options, she decided to keep moving forward in the wrong direction, with the rest of the crowd. Since I was not in charge of the students, I allowed them to continue in the wrong direction.

Later that day, I saw the student again and asked, "Were you able to get out of the building okay?"

She replied that her class had actually gotten stuck in the stairwell and that they were reprimanded by administration for using the wrong exit.

I inquired as to why she didn't listen when I tried to direct her in the right direction, and again she said, "Well, that's the way that everyone else was going."

I saw the opportunity for a teachable moment and explained to the student that just as in life, although it may seem like the natural thing to do, we shouldn't always follow the crowd.

This situation was an important metaphor for life. Many people are living and moving in the direction of the crowd, even if means going against their heart and God's divine will. This is not necessarily because they think that it is the right direction, but rather because they simply cannot muster the courage to go their own way.

The King and the Poisoned Well

The following is a parable from an unknown author. I have seen various versions of the story, but it goes something like this:

> *"There once was a king who ruled over a vast kingdom. He was feared for his might and loved for his wisdom. Now in the heart of the city there was a well with pure and crystalline waters from which all of the inhabitants drank. When all were asleep, an evil wizard entered the city and poured seven drops of a strange liquid into the well. Anyone who drank from the contaminated well would go mad.*
>
> *"The next day, all the people drank the water, but not the king. And the people began to say, 'The king is mad and has lost his reason. Look how strangely he behaves. We cannot be ruled by a madman, so he must be destroyed.'*
>
> *"The king grew very fearful, for his subjects were preparing to rise against him. He prepared to leave the city, but the Queen stopped him saying, 'Let us drink from the well, then we will be the same as they are.'*
>
> *"And so they drank from the communal well of madness, and then became as insane as their*

*subjects. The next day, there was great rejoic-
ing among the people, for their beloved king had
finally regained his reason, and he was allowed to
rule in peace over his people for the rest of his days"
(Author unknown).*

Why would the king drink the poisoned water if he knew that
it would cause him to go mad? The king made the conscious decision
to go mad rather than be questioned and possibly overthrown by
his people. It seems like the obvious wrong decision, but in today's
world, many people have done this very same thing. Despite the fact
that some notions and beliefs seem illogical, rather than be considered strange or different by their peers, many accept the beliefs of
the majority. For many, it is better to be wrong, than to be on the
outside. This way of thinking is dangerous. Blind obedience opens
the door for manipulation and violence.

Therefore, it is imperative that you stand strong in your beliefs.
Don't be a part of the problem just to appease those who may disagree
with you. I challenge you to be courageous and think for yourself!

The Power of the Pen

It is no secret that the mainstream media can make or break an individual or organization. It is for this very reason that it is essential
that we take control and free our minds from the mental and spiritual manipulation we have all been subjected to, whether we've been
aware of it or not.

If we are to ever truly be happy in this life, we need to take
the time think about, analyze, and educate ourselves on matters that
inevitably have an impact on our lives. A truly confident individual
is not afraid to stand up and reject absurdities that are forced upon

them by mass marketing at every turn. It is absolutely critical that you become an independent thinker!

Expand Your Knowledge

One of the greatest aspects of being a history teacher was that it not only allowed but also required me to expand my knowledge about history, as well as the current state of world affairs.

As with most careers, we become somewhat of an authority in our chosen field. For example, my sister works in the medical field, and as a result, she is very familiar with the health-care system and medical terminology, as well as various medical treatments. When she speaks about work, much of what she says sounds foreign to me.

With that being said, becoming a teacher gave me the opportunity to delve into the lives and backgrounds of some of the most interesting events and individuals throughout history.

Teaching was a perfect fit for my personality. I've always had an inquisitive nature and always wondered why things were the way that they were, as well as how things worked the way that they did. From automobiles to the elaborate social structures and inner workings of various societies and cultures, I wanted to understand how things worked.

As a teacher, I would examine the various countries, cultures, and events throughout history and see what worked for them and what didn't. I would oftentimes find myself playing the what-if game. For example, I would ask myself questions such as, "What if JFK had not been assassinated," or "What would have happened if communism had triumphed?"

I would try to imagine myself living during a particular time period or put myself in the shoes of the individual I was reading, learning, or teaching about. I always wanted to know as much as possible so that I could elaborate on topics while lecturing, but also because I was genuinely interested.

As I continued to study, learn, and teach, my worldview gradually began to change. Through my studies, I was able to vastly increase my knowledge about the various religious beliefs and governmental structures of the world. I learned about their origins and the major events that have occurred and in turn shaped global affairs as we know them today. Oftentimes I would begin to research a particular topic and find myself, hours later, still meticulously digesting details.

As my knowledge continued to expand, my understanding continued to grow, and as a result, my perspective on the world, as well as life, continued to evolve. This continued expansion offered me the opportunity to attain a number of realizations about the interconnectedness of the world and its inhabitants.

I felt as though I could make honest assessments and form my own opinions on major global issues rather than just blindly accepting what I was being fed by news and media outlets, which oftentimes report the news with a biased agenda.

I felt more aware and confident when engaging in discussions, as well as in my life in general. I came to a realization about the importance of taking responsibility for your life and putting a genuine effort toward educating oneself. In the world that we live in today, you cannot afford to allow yourself to be manipulated and coerced in regard to how you live and how you think by outside sources. In the past, people have allowed themselves to be manipulated by outside sources, and the results were proven to be disastrous.

Learn to love learning. Learn to love to improve yourself. Find joy in growing as a human being in all facets of your life. Seek out information in virtually all aspects of life. Learn about science, religion, culture, philosophy, and any other topic that piques your interest. By doing this, you will be able to live a more fulfilling life. After some time has passed, when you look back at your former self and see the personal growth that you've experienced, I promise you that you will not be sorry.

Why So Sad?

The United States is the most abundant nation on the face of the earth. Today, Americans enjoy better living standards than at any other time in our nation's great history.

It seems logical then that we should be happier and more fulfilled than we could possibly imagine. Unfortunately, that is simply not the case. As a matter of fact, the sad truth is that if you were to ask for a sincere answer from many Americans about their level of happiness, they would tell you that they feel sad, frustrated, and unfulfilled.

A logical person would ask, "How could people be sad and unfulfilled in a land with so much opportunity and abundance?"

The answer is simple. It is because most people are not truly in control of their own minds, thoughts, and beliefs, and therefore they are not in control of their own lives.

It is true that in certain circumstances conformity is acceptable and even necessary, but most Americans are conforming to the wrong ways of thinking and living.

Therefore, the more that you educate yourself and the more knowledge that you acquire, the more capable you will become to break free from the sadness that many people are currently enduring.

You will, in turn, become an independent thinker, which will allow you to decide what will make you happy, rather than allowing outside sources to dictate your thoughts.

Once this occurs, there is nothing that you cannot do. This is precisely why the British philosopher Francis Bacon once stated, "Knowledge is power."

And the best news is that any one and every one of us is capable of continuing our growth in knowledge and wisdom. And due to the access of information that is available through the use of technology today, there is no limit on the amount of growth that you can experience as a human being.

Limitless

Despite being told since elementary school that we can do anything that we put our minds to, most people carry a tremendous amount of doubt regarding their capabilities throughout their life.

Most of us spend the majority of our time with individuals from similar backgrounds and with similar expectations. I'm certainly not suggesting that there is anything wrong with spending time with friends, but what I'm saying is that we will only live up to the expectations that are put in place by ourselves and those that we associate with. Most people will never rise above the level of expectation that they have become accustomed to.

Many people simply cannot envision themselves accomplishing things that are considered extraordinary by most standards, not because they're not capable of doing so but because they have set their sights far lower than what they're actually capable of achieving.

We tend to look at successful people and think that they either inherited their position in life or caught some sort of break that catapulted them to the top with little or no effort. We often think that there is no way that an ordinary person such as ourselves could ever rise to the heights of those that, by most standards, are considered to be extremely successful.

But what we need to realize is that the individuals who have reached great levels of success are simply ordinary people who have achieved extraordinary things. The majority of highly successful people are no different than you or I. They've had to work tremendously hard to get where they are today. It's just that we didn't witness their climb to the top firsthand. We are unaware of the challenges that were overcome, the sacrifices that were made, and the hours that were spent laboring in order for those individuals to achieve their goals.

What Are You Doing While No One Is Watching?

One of my favorite quotes in regard to putting in the time and effort required in order to achieve goals comes from none other than the boxing great Muhammad Ali. Ali was once quoted as saying, "The fight is won or lost far away from witnesses—behind the lines, in the gym, and out there on the road, long before I dance under those lights."

Ali was known for his ability to shine when the lights were on, winning some of boxing's most exciting fights. Many people probably thought that he didn't need to work very hard, and that much of his success could be attributed to natural ability. But just like many who are successful in the athletic realm, in entertainment, or in business, there are many hours dedicated to the craft long before success is reached. So therefore I ask you, what are you doing to achieve your goals when nobody is watching? Are you genuinely doing all that you can to create the type of life that you desire? Goals are not achieved without effort. Therefore, it is imperative that you take it upon yourself to put forth the necessary effort at all times to create the life of your dreams.

Expect Success

Have you ever heard the saying "The rich get richer and the poor get poorer?" Although it may seem unfair, it does seem as though those who are successful and wealthy continue to grow in their wealth and success, and they tend to pass it on to their descendants who then seem to continue to do the same.

But contrary to popular belief, people who are wealthy and successful do not grow in their wealth due to the fact that they are more intelligent, more capable, or even because their wealth was handed down. Rather, the reason that individuals who have reached a higher station in life continue to rise higher is because that is precisely what they expect to happen.

You see, I had a friend once whose father was a self-made millionaire. My friend and I used to run around together, and at times, we would interact with adults who were older, more respected, and sometimes even in authoritative positions. But regardless of who we were interacting with, I always noticed that my friend talked and acted as though he expected a certain amount of respect from the individuals with whom we were speaking.

I remember that this fact was evident enough that it caught my attention and made me wonder where this sense of entitlement, for lack of a better term, came from. My friend wasn't rude by any means, but as I've mentioned, he seemed to expect and demand a certain amount of respect from others.

I, on the other hand, came from humble beginnings. My father was a coal miner and although I was very proud of my father's work ethic, I sometimes felt uncertain of myself when associating with those in a position of higher social status.

In my hometown, if a person went to college, it was a significant accomplishment. If they graduated college, it was a tremendous accomplishment. And if they had a successful career, they were a pillar of the community.

But the majority of people that I grew up with didn't go to college, nor was there much of an expectation for them to. When an individual establishes a low standard for themselves, or those who perhaps have had a low expectation placed upon them by a parent or community, they will never rise above that expectation or standard. They will store that low expectation in their subconscious mind, and it will affect every aspect of their lives—from interactions with others to the types of jobs that they will acquire, and even their personal relationships. Therefore, it is imperative that you look at yourself as not only deserving to be successful and happy but also as if it were an inevitability that you will be so. After all, your Heavenly Father created the universe. He has placed greatness on the inside of you and in turn you can expect greatness from yourself!

Following in the Footsteps

The results of expecting success is clearly evident throughout all facets of society. The old saying that "the apple doesn't fall far from the tree" can be applied to the notion of expecting success. It is precisely why you see so many children follow in the footsteps of their parents. If the father is an NFL quarterback, the possibility of this becoming a reality for the child suddenly becomes far more attainable in their own mind. The same goes for police officers, teachers, and so on. This has even been proven to be true for the president of the United States. Once the groundwork has been laid, it becomes simply a matter of following in the footsteps of their parent or role model.

In the family and environment in which my wealthy friend grew up, college was not only an expectation but a requirement. He was expected to go to college, major in business and finance, and eventually take over the family business and continue to thrive. He interacted with and was exposed to individuals of a higher social status his entire life, and so he felt comfortable when conversing with those in the upper echelons of society. Obviously, this puts someone who is not of the same socioeconomic background at a disadvantage, and so I began to realize the absolute importance of holding oneself to a higher standard, regardless of the culture in which one is raised.

We should not only hold ourselves to a higher standard, but we should always work hard and expect to be successful in whatever it is that we are trying to achieve. Stop allowing the quality of your life to be limited by your expectations or the expectations of others and set a new standard for every facet of your life including your education, career, and relationships. Set for yourself an expectation of success and ultimate happiness!

What Type of Person Do You Want to Become?

One of the most commonly overlooked steps necessary toward accomplishing one's goals is to clearly define the type of person that you want to become.

Sometimes the goals that we want to pursue seem clear. Perhaps an individual wants to lose twenty pounds or start their own business. And although these are worthy goals to pursue, it is of vital importance for an individual to clearly define for themselves the type of person that they need to become in order to achieve these goals. In reality, if you are able to become the type of person that you wish to be, you will then be able to follow through and accomplish the goals that you've set for yourself.

Consider this question sincerely, what type of person do you want to become? Have you ever given any thought to the types of characteristics that you admire in a person and whether or not you possess and are currently displaying those types of characteristics? If the answer is no, then this could be severely hindering your quest for happiness. It is of vital importance for you to realize one thing: *you are capable of becoming the type of person that you want to become!*

This bears repeating, you are capable of becoming the type of person that you and everyone else can not only respect but also admire! You have the capability inside of you to develop and express the qualities that are ever present in successful, happy people.

But in order for you to become that person, you must first sit down, think about, and write down the qualities and characteristics that you want to possess and exhibit. Some suggestions might include but are not limited to *loving, kind, generous, grateful, hardworking, caring, resilient,* perserverant,, *determined, open-minded, articulate, inquisitive, thoughtful, disciplined, optimistic,* and *happy.* This list may help get you started but feel free to indulge and write as many characteristics and qualities that come to mind.

Once you have identified the type of person that you want to become, you are well on your way to actualizing that dream and becoming that person. It is imperative for you to look at, read over, and remind yourself of the qualities that you wish to possess each day. You will find that gradually, with each passing day, you will continue to grow into and become the very person in which you have defined and envisioned.

Are You Primed for Happiness?

In his widely popular book *Blink*, author Malcolm Gladwell discusses a psychological term known as *priming*. The term is derived from the idea of priming in regard to something mechanical, such as an engine or an old style of pump. For example, before starting an engine, you may prime it or fill the carburetor with fuel before ignition in order to ensure a smoother start-up.

In regard to psychological priming, Gladwell refers to using specific words in order to prime or prepare your "adaptive unconscious" for whichever type of mental state that you are trying to create. Gladwell cites an experiment conducted by psychologists John Bargh, Mark Chen, and Lara Burrows on priming in which they would utilize something called a "scramble-test."

They would assign one group of test subjects to take the scramble-test and infuse it with words that would be considered negative, such as *aggressive, bold, rude, bother, disturb, intrude,* and *infringe.*

A second group of test subjects would be subjected to the same type of test, except this time, they set out to prime the subject with words that would be considered positive, such as *respect, considerate, appreciate, patiently, yield, polite,* and *courteous.*

After the students finished the test, they were then tasked with walking down the hallway in order to receive instructions for the next step of the experiment from the experiment coordinator. All the while, unknowingly to the subject, this actually *was* the next part of the experiment.

Little did they know that upon arriving at the assigned room in order to inquire as to the next step of the experiment, the doorway would be blocked by an individual that was staged to appear to be immersed in a conversation with the individual from whom the subject was to receive their orders.

As you can probably guess, the students that were primed with the negative words interrupted the conversation after about five minutes on average. After all, the seeds of negativity had been planted beforehand during the scramble-test; therefore, the stage was set, and their mind was primed for a negative interaction.

On the other hand, of the subjects that were primed to be polite with the positive words, 82 percent never interrupted at all! Just as in the case with the students who were negatively primed, when the opportunity for the positive seeds that were planted earlier had the chance to blossom, they responded to the situation in a much more patient, positive manner (Gladwell, 52–55).

There is an invaluable lesson for all of us to take away from this experiment. This experiment quantitatively demonstrates the very wisdom that was spoken in the book of Galatians millennia earlier, which states, "Whatever a man sows, he will also reap." Despite being written a long time ago, the Bible is speaking precisely about priming. You see when a farmer sows or plants a seed, although it may take some time, he will reap or harvest the crop in which he had planted. In turn, if he plants corn, he will reap corn. If he sows wheat, he'll harvest wheat, and so on.

The same can be said for the very seeds or thoughts that we plant in our mind on a daily basis. If you plant negative seeds or prime your mind negatively, you will most likely experience negative interactions. On the other hand, if you prime your mind in a positive fashion, or in other words if you plant positive seeds, you will most likely experience positive interactions throughout the day. This was made evident in the priming experiment.

The truth of the matter is that many of us today are simply not priming our minds for a happy life. Although we want to reap happiness, we unknowingly sabotage our yield by sowing the wrong seeds.

Many of you reading this can relate. Oftentimes the first thoughts and words that come to mind upon waking up in the morning are littered with negativity. Immediately, when the alarm goes off, we oftentimes find ourselves angry at the thought of getting out of bed. This momentum continues to build as we go about our morning routine when thoughts of not wanting to go to work bombard our subconscious mind. We begin to think about the day ahead and sometimes continue to focus on stressful deadlines and annoying coworkers.

By the time we're in our car, we're well on our way to a bad day. We get angry at traffic, and the momentum continues to build. By the time we arrive at work, our minds, as well as our day, have become thoroughly primed for negativity, and oftentimes we see that negativity play itself out. The negative seeds come to fruition throughout the day, through our daily actions and interactions.

Oftentimes, this continues to happen day in and day out, week after week, month after month, year after year, with intermittent breaks sprinkled in through vacations, weekends, and holidays. Before we know it, this negative priming of our mind has created an angry, negative, unhappy life.

The good news is that this doesn't have to your reality. As a matter of fact, it is completely in your power to do the exact opposite and prime your mind with positive thoughts.

If you truly desire to live a happy life, then it is up to you to, immediately upon waking up in the morning, begin the day on a positive note. Some of you may ask, "Well, how do I do that?" You can accomplish this by basically doing the opposite of what you may be doing now.

For example, as soon as you turn off the alarm clock, rather than starting the day with that first negative thought of not wanting to get out of bed, thank the Lord for His love and for the amazing blessings He has bestowed upon you. Thank Him for your health and the fact that you are *able* to get out of bed. Thank Him for the blessing of employment and the ability to go to work. Continue to build this momentum throughout your morning routine. Sing songs of praise. Focus on the positive aspects of your life. Think about the positive goals that you wish to pursue. Read over your goals and the characteristics that you wish to possess. Expect to have a great day.

On the way to work, do not allow yourself to be frustrated by traffic. Rather, remind yourself that getting frustrated will not solve anything but instead will increase your stress level and blood pressure. Say a prayer while driving or listen to your favorite pastor or motivational audio recordings.

Now that your mind is thoroughly primed, carry this positive mind-set through the rest of your day. And don't forget to smile. Remember that the expression that you display to others will most times be reciprocated. If you smile, you will most likely receive a smile in return.

I promise you that if you conduct your morning routine in this manner, the events and interactions of your day will be much more pleasant and rewarding. Continue to do this day after day, week after week, month after month, and year after year. Before you know it, you will be able to look back on the years of your life with a sigh and a smile and be sincerely grateful to have lived such an amazing life.

Stronger Than You Can Imagine!

If you are sincere about achieving a happy life, then it is time that you give yourself credit where credit is due. Just like our favorite figures from the Bible, including Moses and David, you too were created by the Heavenly Father. He has instilled in you too talents and abilities that you have long forgotten about or even perhaps never even realized that you possessed.

It's time for you to take a good look in the mirror and not just realize but also acknowledge that you are capable of greatness. It's time to free your mind from the mental restraints that have been holding you back in life. It's time to unveil to the world, the successful person that dwells within you.

Whether you want to finish college, improve your marriage, write a book, or paint a work of art, if you have felt a calling or yearning on the inside to pursue a particular goal, that's your Heavenly Father encouraging you to take a chance. Stop allowing yourself to waste time and pursue the endeavors that will give meaning to your life. He knows that you are capable and strong enough to accomplish whatever dream He has put in your heart. Whenever you begin to question yourself, lean on your Heavenly Father for strength. For as Philippians 4:13 (NIV) states, "I can do all things through Him who gives me strength."

Silence the Negative Voices

Like I've mentioned previously in this book, most of us at some point in our lives were put down by someone. Perhaps it was an acquaintance, a friend, or even a loved one.

Many of us have been told that we're not capable enough, smart enough, or just plain not good enough. We've been told that there is no way that we could ever go out and accomplish our dreams.

Unfortunately, many people allow these negative comments to take root in their hearts and minds, and they begin to believe those naysayers. Before they know it, they've decided that those people are probably right, and they give up on pursuing their dreams just when they're getting started or maybe even before trying.

Have you ever been talked out of pursuing a dream? I urge you to realize that insults and criticism oftentimes stem from envy. We've all heard the old adage that "misery loves company." A great deal of truth can be found in this saying.

You see, many people feel frustrated, angry, and disappointed about the way that their lives have gone or are going. This frustration breeds feelings of negativity. Therefore, when frustrated people see someone with the strength and courage to move forward and pursue a better life, they feel resentment because they themselves do not possess the strength or courage to do so.

In turn, they will do everything in their power to see that someone else who is living in the same environment does not rise up and find the happiness that they so desperately desire. They will oftentimes do everything in their power to sabotage another person's success.

Olympic wrestler and bronze medalist Nate Carr once said, "Hurting people, hurt people." This message is short but yet very profound because it is truly those who are hurting inside that seek to bring others down by inflicting pain. It is for this very reason that bullying has been rampant throughout the centuries. Bullies are nothing more than people who are miserable on the inside and therefore look to inflict misery upon others so that they are not the only one experiencing pain.

Jesus Knew the Importance of Protecting His Mind

Consider the fact that if you achieve your goals, others may feel less than adequate because perhaps they have not yet achieved their goals or, worse yet, they never had the courage or ambition to get started.

Jesus knew the importance of not allowing others to plant seeds of doubt in His mind. That is precisely why when the disciple Peter suggested that maybe Jesus should not follow through on His divine purpose, Jesus rebuked him, exclaiming, "Get behind me Satan!" (Matthew 16:23)

Jesus had a task before Him that you and I could not possibly fathom, yet even the Messiah knew that if He allowed even one ounce of doubt to penetrate His mind, His path could be diverted, Satan could overcome, and humanity would be lost.

Steel Your Mind

Obviously, the stakes aren't so high in your case, but your happiness and success are on the line nonetheless. That is exactly why it is so important that you build a fortress around your mind and protect it from those who want to keep you from the amazing life that you are capable of achieving.

If you find yourself as the target of criticism or negative comments, you must not allow these thoughts to infiltrate and negatively affect your mind-set. Block the negative thoughts by reaffirming in your mind the positive goals that you wish to achieve. Remind yourself of the person that you are to become.

If it is a particular individual that is mocking or speaking negatively about your heart's desire, you may unfortunately be forced to distance yourself from them.

You need to be aware of the fact that there will be people in your life who will doubt you and tell you that your goals are impossible. Remember the words of Jesus Himself when He stated, "Through God all things are possible." (Matthew 19:26) Do not allow the words or negativity of others to sabotage your quest for happiness and success. Steel your mind!

It's Time to Break Free

Have you ever found yourself in a situation where you were following the crowd despite feeling in your heart that it may not be right? It's time to stop being an adherent to the world's way of thinking. It's time to free your mind from the desires, thoughts, ideas, and beliefs that have been holding you back in life. It's time to become an independent thinker! Find enjoyment and fulfillment in the process of questioning, learning, investigating, educating, and, most importantly, thinking for yourself. Once you begin to do this, you will truly be in control of your own life, and, in turn, you will also be in control of your own level of happiness.

Trust in the guidance that your Heavenly Father is speaking into your heart, and you will always find yourself walking the path of independence, fulfillment, joy, love, and ultimate happiness.

Free Your Mind

Stop allowing the negativity from others to sabotage your life. Happiness and success can become a reality for you. Your potential is limitless but can only be utilized if you apply step 5 and *free your mind.*

STEP 6

Let Go

"This is where your liberation is found."

Check Your Bags

Do you ever feel overwhelmed, like the weight of the world is on your shoulders? Have you ever felt anxious, like no matter how much you accomplish, you never seem to be done? Do you carry around a sense of guilt regarding family or friends, as if you simply aren't living up to the expectations of others? If you're like most people, then you're more than likely carrying around a lot of weight. I'm not referring to physical weight, but rather emotional weight. The truth is that many of us have continued to compile a significant amount of emotional baggage throughout the years. And just like physical weight, emotional weight can weigh us down and prevent us from attaining the happiness that we so desperately desire.

In a world full of abundance and opportunity, Americans should be more carefree and happy than ever before. Unfortunately, we all know that that simply is not the case. As a matter of fact, stress levels in the United States are at an all-time high. High blood pressure, obesity, and stomach ulcers are more common than ever, and all result from feeling overly stressed.

Many of us continue to go about our lives day after day, overwhelmed and stressed, with a feeling that we can never seem to allow ourselves to relax. If you can relate to these feelings of being overwhelmed and stressed, then you simply need to do one thing—let go!

Reconnect with Your Spiritual Self

I believe that every human being possesses two sides. First, there is the earthly side. This is the side of our being that goes to work, pays the bills, mows the lawn, and coaches our child's soccer team. This side is essential for our survival and is necessary due to the fact that we wouldn't be able to function in the modern world without it.

The second side of our being is our spiritual side. This is the side of our being that is responsible for serving and loving our Heavenly Father, loving others, as well as loving ourselves. It is also responsible for the feeling of love and interconnectedness that flows throughout all of humanity.

Both of these sides are important and essential for our very survival. But as time has passed and technology and innovation have progressed, many people have become tremendously imbalanced between the two. The continuing trend is that many people have placed more emphasis on their earthy self and, as a result, have become more disconnected with their spiritual self. If you can relate to this notion, then it is of vital importance that you make the effort to create balance between your earthly and spiritual sides.

Material Wealth *Does Not* Equal Happiness

I was once watching a popular daytime television talk show. The show was hosting a couple who had been married for a number of years, but the two simply were not happy in their current marriage situation. The most frustrating part was that they couldn't figure out why.

As I was watching the show, the woman in the relationship said something to the effect of, "We have a beautiful home, nice cars, go on vacation every year, but we are still not happy."

I remember thinking to myself upon hearing the lady explain her situation that her explanation of where she expected to find happiness was the very problem. Many people are in the same exact mind-set as the couple on the show. They believe that their happiness will be found in wealth and material possessions. But the truth of the matter is that this is a shallow, superficial worldview. True joy and happiness must be found in something much more meaningful. I'm certainly not suggesting that you shouldn't possess those types of things or go on annual vacations, but what I am advocating is that if you think that possessions and vacations will provide you automatic happiness, you will inevitably find yourself as frustrated and unhappy as the couple on the show.

Many people have been conditioned through advertising and marketing to believe that their goals and ambitions should be geared toward monetary wealth and the acquisition of material possessions. From the time that we are born, we have been continually told that if we do not work more in order to make more money so that we can buy the latest high-definition television or cell phone, we will be missing out, and our lives will be found lacking.

It is a well-known fact that corporations spend billions of dollars on marketing in order to create clever commercials and advertising campaigns. They go to great lengths to secure contracts in order to ensure that the most famous celebrities or athletes are endorsing their products.

We are told that we *need* to go on luxury cruises and get a new car every two years in order to prove to the world that we have reached a particular level of status in life.

We have been told time and again by the multitudes of advertisements and commercials that the way to attain happiness is through material wealth.

It is imperative if you are to ever achieve lifelong happiness that you grasp the following statement: *Despite what you've been told to believe your entire life, you must let go of the notion that the acquisition of monetary wealth and material possessions is a surefire way to attain true happiness.*

You should not feel silly or like a fool for believing this notion. After all, you and anyone who has been born and raised in the modern world have been conditioned to believe the very same thing.

Let Go and Stop Seeking Short-Lived Happiness

Can you ever remember a time in your life when there was something that you "just had to have?" I once saw a bumper sticker that read, "He who dies with the most toys wins." We've been groomed from the time that we're infants to believe that the more "toys" that you have, the better your quality of life. But if you are sincerely honest about the purchases that you've made in the past, whether a new sweater, a pair of shoes, or television, you will most likely recall that although the initial purchase may have been somewhat exhilarating, that feeling deteriorated relatively quickly.

The truth is that as the days and weeks passed, so did the feeling of excitement. Before long, you felt the yearning to go buy another sweater or pair of shoes, and so the cycle continued until you accumulated a closet full of sweaters and shoes that you haven't worn in years. There is no shame in this. We've all done the same thing to some degree in our lives. Some will even continue doing this for the rest of their life here on earth, only to end up broke, with a gnawing sense of emptiness and an ever-present void on the inside.

I'm certainly not suggesting that you give up all your money and personal possessions. If you are going to live comfortably in the modern world, you will need money for sustenance, a car to drive to work, and a phone for obvious reasons, etc.

I'm simply saying that you need to raise your awareness to the fact that keeping up with the Joneses and acquiring more possessions simply does not result in more happiness.

Let Go and Stop Placing Undue Stress on Yourself

Have you ever stopped and taken a closer look at the things that you are stressed out about? If you were to do so, I believe that you would realize that although there are areas in your life that need your attention, most of the things that you worry about on a daily basis are not a matter of life or death. As a matter of fact, a great deal of the stress that many of us feel today is exaggerated and self-imposed. What I mean by this is that many of us put a great deal of pressure on ourselves strictly because we're concerned with the image that we are portraying to others.

For example, you may want to buy a new car even though the car that you currently own runs great simply because you feel that you would be happier driving the newer model so that others might be impressed. Advertisers go to great lengths and hire well-known celebrities to drive their cars in commercials to add an air of wealth and status to their brand. The commercials are geared toward making you feel as though that very same prestige and feeling of confidence would then be conveyed upon you if you were driving their brand. And while it may be nice to drive a brand-new car, you will also acquire a brand-new car payment, which many times does not coincide with an individual's income level.

Another example is that maybe you feel the need to get that newer, bigger television despite the fact that your current television works completely fine. But still the desire persists so that when the guys come over to watch the game, they will be completely blown away and impressed by your new purchase.

Oftentimes these purchases push our credit to the limit and result in many living from paycheck to paycheck, with the worry of running out of finances constantly lingering in the back of their minds. According to an article on Time.com, on average, an American between the ages of 18-65 has $4,717 of credit card debt. It goes on to state that the #1 reason for carrying that debt is "availability." This means that since the credit is offered, many Americans simply cannot muster up the discipline to reject the offer and go on to use the credit for unnecessary purchases. Millions of people literally stress their wallets, as well as their peace of mind, to the max in a desperate attempt to attain happiness.

Money Is Fine, *but* It Is Not the Answer

This isn't simply about living beyond your means. It's more about the notion that more is better. It's about letting go of the conditioning that we've been subjected to for most of our lives that we need to accumulate a great deal of "stuff."

You can be the wealthiest person on the planet and have all the glitz and glam that money can buy, but if you are not in alignment with God and receiving the spiritual nourishment that every human being not only desires but absolutely needs, you will not be fulfilled, and you will not be happy.

Let's take a minute to think about this logically. If money was the only requisite for happiness, then once an individual attains a million dollars or so, they should be as happy as can be, but as we all know, this simply is not true. As a matter of fact, there are currently many people living in this world with millions and even billions of dollars in their bank accounts that are downright miserable.

This is precisely why we see so many celebrities and athletes with huge amounts of money at their disposal addicted to drugs and alcohol. These wealthy individuals live in extravagant homes, have more clothes than they could wear in a lifetime, and own enough cars to drive a different one each day of the week, yet many are severely depressed, turning to drugs or alcohol for relief. Unfortunately, some find themselves in rehab or sometimes even tragically overdosing as a result.

A person of average wealth would look at some of these people and think, "What could they possibly have to be sad about? They have all of the money they could ever want." The answer is that there is still a void inside that remains unfilled.

There Is Only *One* Solution

There is only one thing that can fix this problem. There is only one solution that can fill this void that many feel inside, and that is the love of our Heavenly Father.

No amount of drugs, alcohol, promiscuity, or any other earthly pleasure can give you the fulfillment, the sense of peace, joy, and, ultimately, the happiness that you can attain from loving and serving the Father. Many have and will continue to try, but God's love is the only answer.

A Lesson from the Wealthiest Man to Have Ever Lived

Have you ever dreamed about what you would buy if you were rich? Have you ever thought about how your life would be different if money were no object? In the biblical book of Ecclesiastes 1:14, King Solomon discusses the frustration caused by trying to fill the void in his heart by indulging in earthly pleasures.

You see, King Solomon was not only the wisest but also the wealthiest man to have ever lived. His riches surpassed anything that you or I could ever imagine.

In Ecclesiastes 1:9, Solomon discusses his pursuit of happiness through earthly pleasures by what he refers to as "chasing the wind." He lists all his earthly endeavors including the construction of many palaces, his multitude of wives and concubines, his search for happiness through laughter brought about by his court jesters, and even through the consumption of wine.

Despite his best efforts, King Solomon only found himself frustrated and with a void still remaining in his soul.

Solomon eventually came to realize that nothing "under the Sun" could fill the emptiness that he felt inside and that there was only one solution to his frustration, and that was the divine love of his Heavenly Father.

When I first read Solomon's account, it had an air of familiarity. It reminded me of the many stories that frequent the news regarding celebrities and well-known individuals that continually find themselves in trouble. Many of us are guilty of the same offense, trying desperately to fill the void in our soul with material possessions and earthly pleasures.

Our ways of seeking happiness tend to vary from individual to individual. Some spend until they can spend no more, others may find comfort in food, and still others may turn to television, video games, or social media. In extreme cases, alcohol and drugs are used in order to numb ourselves from the stresses of life.

Oftentimes we try to rationalize, thinking to ourselves that if we can make more money and buy more, maybe that will do the trick. We purchase bigger homes and more expensive cars and boats and go on vacations until we can purchase no more, ironically, only to be left with more utter frustration, disappointment, and massive debt. Inevitably the debt leads to even more stress, and the vicious cycle continues.

It's time that we come to the realization that if King Solomon, the wisest and wealthiest man to have ever lived, could not fill the void in his soul with the hundreds of mansions, partners, laughter, or wine, then we too could never fill the void with such things.

And just like King Solomon, every one of us has access, at this very moment, to the only solution guaranteed to alleviate the emptiness inside, and that is the love of our Heavenly Father.

Happiness without God Is Impossible

Newspapers, tabloids, and television are jam-packed today with stories of celebrities and other wealthy individuals who have made bad choices in their lives and, as a result, have found themselves facing insurmountable difficulty. One lesson that these news stories reveals to us is that despite their fame, celebrities are simply normal human beings and therefore are at risk of suffering the same types of hardships as everyone else.

Please do not misunderstand what I'm saying here. I'm certainly not passing judgment on those who have become lost despite achieving a high level of success. I feel a tremendous amount of sympathy upon hearing the news of the latest celebrity divorce, stint in rehab, or even death. Most of us would tend to think that these individuals have immense amounts of finances at their disposal and are most likely living the ideal lifestyle.

But in reality, many celebrities are living with the same type of disillusion and frustration as many ordinary people, despite their wealth. What we must realize is that most celebrities start their lives out as ordinary people with dreams and aspirations of achieving success. They work hard through the years, sacrifice, sometimes barely making ends meet, continuing to struggle as they climb the ladder. All the while, they're thinking in their mind that once they "make it," they will live the rest of their life in perpetual bliss.

And then it happens, they get their big break, or the hard work finally pays off. Suddenly, they are no longer an ordinary person. Rather, they are now famous and, even better, rich. People want their autographs, they are getting paid huge sums of money for their work, and oftentimes they receive elaborate gifts that they had never dreamed they would receive. They have friends coming out of the woodwork. The hard work has paid off, and it seems as though the struggle and strife of life are gone forever.

Everything is amazing, for a while, but then little by little, it happens. It starts with a small voice in the back of their mind. It is their old acquaintances, discontentment and emptiness. The individual finds themselves surprised. They thought that the negativity would be gone forever. After all, they've worked hard. They've earned this happiness. Money is no longer an issue. Vacations, forget it. Life is now one big vacation. They should be happier now than ever before.

But they're not, and it doesn't make sense. Isn't this what they've wanted their entire life? Money and fame, a never-ending party? Then why does the happiness seem to be fading?

The discontent that they feel is the same discontent that plagues ordinary people. The fact of the matter is this, if you do not have God in your life, then no matter how much money you have, no matter how much fame and success you have achieved, you simply cannot and will not find happiness. There is absolutely nothing wrong with attaining material wealth. But we must find a deeper meaning and purpose in our lives. This is precisely the reason that we see so many celebrities that seem to have it all fall prey to tragedy

Let Go of Life-Wasting Activities

We're all entitled to a little rest and relaxation every now and again. Many of us are extremely busy, and work can be exhausting. Perhaps you need to unwind for a bit when you get home after a long day.

Or maybe you've had a stressful week full of chaos and non-stop activity. At the end of the week, you've earned a day or two to unwind and rejuvenate.

Although the desire to relax is perfectly understandable and absolutely necessary, we need to be careful not to get lost in "life-wasting activities." What I'm referring to when I speak of life-wasting activities are the activities and endeavors that have become an unknowingly dangerous part of many peoples daily lives that can tragically lead to us wasting a significant portion of our time here on earth.

Activities such as playing video or online games, watching television or movies, and using social media can literally become addictive and keep you from pursuing meaningful goals and possibly cost you your chance at true happiness.

As I've mentioned previously, I'm not suggesting that you need to completely remove these activities from your life. Perhaps one or more of these types of activities are a part of your life that you genuinely enjoy.

But when you make an honest assessment of the amount of time per day, week, or month that is spent on these obsessions and realize that they are consuming a significant amount of your time, then it is essential that you take control and let go of these activities from your life.

Taking time for yourself to relax is of vital importance. Of course you need to maintain an outlet for stress and find time for recreation, but far too often, many people intend on only spending a few minutes to check their favorite social media site or to play a quick game or two on their favorite game console, only to find themselves still behind the screen two or more hours later. If this is a regular occurrence in your life, then I reiterate, you need to stop handing control of your life to these activities that will be of absolutely no benefit to you or your happiness in the long run.

Don't Get Caught Up

At one point in my life, I had unintentionally fallen into a routine of getting home from work day after day, and before even getting out of my work clothes, I would turn on the game console and start playing. I had every intention of only finishing a game or two.

But before I knew it, an hour or more had passed before I finally snapped out of my trance and decided to turn the game off and go about more productive activities.

This routine went on for a number of months until I finally came to the realization of how much time was being wasted playing a game that was going to result in absolutely no benefit to my life. I stopped myself cold turkey, and haven't played any video games since.

Imagine what would happen if you took all the time that is wasted on social media, video games, or similar mindless activities and put it toward something constructive. You could possibly start a business, get healthy, write a book, expand your knowledge on virtually anything and everything, or pursue some other worthwhile endeavor that would genuinely be beneficial to your life. This could be life-changing!

Time Is Precious

Oftentimes we try to use hobbies and recreation as a means to escape reality. Unfortunately, the activities that we are using to try to relieve stress oftentimes result in the exact opposite.

There are numerous stories of cyberbullying and gossip running rampant through social media. With the increased use of technology in our lives, scams such as "catfishing" and identity theft are occurring more and more frequently and are becoming serious problems for many.

As for video games, my blood pressure would be through the roof at times while being caught up in playing my favorite game. I remember times when I was so fired up after finishing a game that I would have difficulty sleeping.

These activities oftentimes lead to the neglecting of personal relationships and priorities, as well as procrastination, which inevitably adds even more stress to our already hectic lives.

If you are truly sincere in pursuing a life full of happiness and fulfillment, you must discipline yourself and seriously consider limiting the amount of time spent on these life-wasting activities, or perhaps even possibly eliminating them from your life altogether. The time that you will attain through the limiting or eliminating of these activities will allow you to focus on more meaningful endeavors.

Let Go of the Past

Have you ever found yourself experiencing a case of the what-ifs? Or has there ever been a time when if you could do anything, you would go back and change past decisions? If so, you are not alone.

An unfortunate fact is that many people today spend a significant amount of time thinking about, reliving, or regretting the past. Oftentimes people simply cannot let go of events that have transpired in their lives, and some even feel a sense of guilt about events that have played out long ago.

The truth of the matter is that you will never be able to live a happy, fulfilling life as long as you are dwelling on the past, whether it was good or bad.

Please do not be confused, I'm certainly not suggesting that you forget about or try to erase memories from your life. There is nothing wrong with analyzing and assessing past experiences for the sake of trying to improve. As a matter of fact, it is necessary to analyze past events and mistakes in order to experience personal growth. During my days as a wrestling coach, I would encourage my athletes to go back and watch video footage of their matches in order to analyze their mistakes, inevitably resulting in improved performance.

But dwelling on the past in self-loathing will only hold you back from the life that you truly want to live.

Leave the Past in the Past

As we go through our lives, we all experience good times and bad. Life is a roller coaster at times. We all have happy experiences and not-so-happy ones. These experiences have shaped who we are as individuals. The problem is that oftentimes people find it difficult to move past those experiences and, as a result, find themselves getting stuck, making it impossible to move forward or to grow.

Whether it's a tough breakup, the loss of a friend, or the falling out with a loved one, many of us tend to cling to that hurtful memory and find it difficult to move past it. Regardless of the fact that most of us have probably experienced more good times than bad, we sometimes make the mistake of focusing on the bad. This is detrimental to attaining a life full of happiness.

Eventually, as we continue to go through life, these negative memories and, more importantly, the negative emotions associated with them accumulate and become like a weight holding us down. Fast-forward about twenty or thirty years and we are now carrying an accumulation of these negative feelings. Before we know it, we're now dragging an enormous amount of guilt, anger, remorse, and sadness behind us in a big bag of negativity. The truth is that if we're unable to let go and cut this bag of negative emotions loose, it can weigh us down and manifest itself through various health problems such as high blood pressure, stomach ulcers, and other ailments.

Oftentimes we try to find an escape or relief from the baggage through the consumption of food, alcohol, social media, or other vices that may not exactly be the best thing for our lives. This is precisely why we need to be aware of the effect that these issues from the past can have on our lives—so we can let go and move forward.

The past can be like an anchor. Just as a ship will remain stationary, unable to move when the anchor is dropped, so will you too remain stationary in life until you learn to let go of past events.

"We should not look back unless it is to derive useful lessons from past errors, and for the purpose of profiting by dearly bought experience" (George Washington).

The Other Side of the Coin

Another reason, and one that can just be just as debilitating, that many tend to hold on to the past is the fact that their past memories are so *good*. Have you ever had a friend who just couldn't stop talking about the "good ol' days"? They have such a feeling of nostalgia about the great memories from the past that they simply cannot let go and constantly refer to things that happened years ago, whether it be the championship game or the beach trip that the gang took after graduating high school.

As mentioned above, this type of thinking can hold you back from the happy life you wish to attain just as much as regretting your past mistakes. I urge you to ask yourself this simple question, "How can you expect to create the best years of your life in the future if you can't stop thinking about the years that are already over?"

A great quote said by Dr. Seuss states this about the past, "Don't cry because it's over. Smile because it happened." Just as Dr. Seuss stated, there is certainly nothing wrong with looking back and remembering past successes and good memories. Just be careful that you are not too busy reminiscing that is distracts you from pursuing your goals and creating the life of your dreams.

Let Go of the Concern of What Others Think

I want to be liked by others. Chances are, you too want to be liked by others as well. Most people want to be liked by others. The truth is that it is completely normal and acceptable for us to want to be liked by others. Most people go through life wanting to have a multitude of people that they can call friends and few, if any, that would be called enemies.

But a concept that is very difficult for many people to grasp is the fact that you are simply not going to click with every person that you meet throughout your life.

This is a concept that I had struggled with for a long time. I've done a considerable amount of traveling and have worked at a number of different jobs throughout my life. I feel that I have relatively good social skills and find that I can get along with most people. Despite these facts, every so often throughout my life, I would meet someone that I simply did not click with.

Like most people, when they meet someone that they do not feel comfortable around, I could sense that something was off. We've probably all gotten that "vibe" at some point. But I didn't feel comfortable with the notion that perhaps someone just didn't seem to care for me.

One coworker in particular comes to mind. He just seemed to have his mind made up from the first time that we had met that he was not going to be my friend. From the time of our initial introduction, I could feel a vibe of negativity toward me emanating from this individual.

My feeling would later be solidified through various negative comments and interactions that we would have throughout our working relationship.

This really bothered me for the first couple of years of working with this individual. Each time we would encounter one another, I would put a big smile on my face and do my best to be as friendly as possible, only to receive an attitude of rudeness and sarcasm in return. It seemed as though the more I felt that this person seemed to dislike me, the harder I would try to change his mind.

Perhaps you have found yourself in a similar situation? Or perhaps you've found yourself on the other side of the situation, where you have met someone who for some reason you just didn't care for from the very inception of your relationship despite your best efforts to feel otherwise?

Regardless, the situation with my coworker continued to bother me for years throughout the time that we had worked together. And then after one particular day, after the individual had thrown a number of negative comments my way, I asked myself a great question that I wished I had thought of sooner. I thought to myself, "Why am I so concerned about what this person thinks? Is it really that important to me that this person would think that I'm a swell guy?"

Get Ahold of Your Ego

And then it hit me, the situation really had nothing to do with the individual liking or disliking me, but rather it had everything to do with my own pride and ego.

I began to realize that this person was the same rank as me. He held no power over me in the workplace hierarchy, and therefore from a work standpoint, there was no legitimate reason as to why it would matter whether or not I was well-liked by this person. I realized that the only reason that it bothered me so much was that it was a blow to my ego.

You see, I, and most people for that matter, tend to believe that if someone does not hold another individual in the highest regard, then that must indicate that there is something wrong with the individual.

If we get the impression that someone dislikes us, we immediately begin to look at ourselves as if something is wrong with or flawed about us. This way of thinking can lead to a feeling of insecurity and lack of self-assuredness.

Sometimes Things Just Don't Click (and That's Okay)

The truth of the matter is that there may or may not be a personality flaw but also that sometimes two people simply do not click.

We've all experienced times where we've initially met someone and you just seemed to hit it off. Things just clicked. You and the other person had plenty of things in common, much to talk about, and the conversation just seemed to flow effortlessly. You could just tell that you and this person were going to become good friends.

Well, in some cases, the complete opposite occurs. Sometimes things just do not click for some reason. The crucial principle for us to understand is that it is okay! We need to be willing to accept the fact that we are not always going to be the best of friends with every-one we meet, and there's absolutely nothing wrong with that.

This certainly doesn't mean that they are right and you are wrong or vice-versa. It simply means that perhaps there's a difference in personality, perspective, or philosophy of life. That's what makes the world go around, and we simply need to accept that fact.

Obviously this isn't an excuse to go through life disregarding your attempt to be friendly and cordial to every individual that you meet. We should always make every effort to be friendly and put our best foot forward when meeting someone new. We should also always, regardless of the situation, show the utmost respect to all human beings.

But what I'm saying is that this simply means that you should let go of the stress and worry attached to a situation where you and another person do not see eye to eye.

The next time you feel down or stressed at the very thought that someone may not like you, take a second and think about this: some of the most amazing and significant individuals to have ever walked the earth had people who absolutely despised them. Individuals such as Martin Luther King Jr., Abraham Lincoln, and even Jesus himself had critics that absolutely loathed their very existence. So when you get the impression that you're not on someone's "favorite persons" list, just remember that you're in good company!

You Simply Can't Please Everyone

Far too often, people spend a great deal of time trying to please others. We've gotten to the point where we've become a nation full of "people pleasers." I'm not suggesting that we should stop being courteous to others or being kind to our fellow human beings, but what I'm suggesting is that we have to recognize that our attempts at making everyone in our lives happy can sometimes rob us of our own happiness.

It's Okay to Be a Bit Selfish

Have you ever known someone, perhaps the selfless mother, grandmother, or aunt who refuses to sit down and eat during Christmas dinner, putting everyone else's needs before her own? Perhaps you are one of those individuals. If so, I commend you for your selflessness. It is truly an admirable quality. However, we need to realize that sometimes it is okay for us to relax, enjoy ourselves, and do the things that we would like to do in order to ensure our own happiness.

Looking back on some of the previous years in my life, I remember always being concerned with the thought of disappointing others. In a desperate attempt to ensure that I was remaining in the good graces of my friends, I was at a party or club every weekend. Despite the fact that it was in direct conflict with the goals that I had put in place for my life, if a friend would call and wanted to head out on the town, I would most of the time oblige.

Eventually I came to the realization that I wasn't being true to myself, and even felt as though I was sacrificing my own goals and happiness because I was spending most of my time and energy trying to please everyone else.

From that moment on, I realized that I needed to be a bit more selfish when it came to making sure that I was on track with what I was trying to accomplish and began doing all that was in my power to stay on the path that God had laid out before me, even it meant disappointing others.

I say this with all due respect, but the fact remains that most of the individuals who are a part of your life are simply not very concerned with whether or not you accomplish your goals. Of course, there are exceptions. At times, there is no stronger supporter than a parent or a loved one who is always there to selflessly offer a ride to practice or an encouraging word toward helping you reach your goals. But for the most part, the majority of people you know are likely not overly concerned with the goals that you've set forth or what you want to attain in life.

Most people are not necessarily out to sabotage your success, but what I'm suggesting is that many times, although a friend may be aware of your desire to accomplish a goal, your goal likely does not take precedence over what that individual wants out of your relationship.

Therefore, it is of the utmost importance that you maintain your discipline when tempted with the chance to put something off until later or become distracted by endeavors that are not in your best interest. It is imperative that you hold yourself accountable and continue moving forward toward the life that you are determined to create for yourself.

I encourage you too to take a look at the people that are a part of your life. Are they supportive in allowing you to live the kind of life that you want to live? Are they understanding when it comes to the pursuit of the goals that you have set for yourself? Or are they holding you back, selfishly concerned only with what they want out of your relationship? Be careful not to be sabotaged by the influence of others. It's tremendously important that we surround ourselves with the right people, stay true to the calling of our own hearts, and pursue the type of life that our Heavenly Father has planned for us.

Let Go

If you are genuine in the pursuit of a happy life, I implore you, stop allowing the weight of the past to hold you back in life. Stop stressing about those with whom you are not the best of friends. Be sure that you are not being led astray by the influence of others. By applying step 6 and allowing yourself to *let go*, you can begin to move forward in life instead of being held back by worry and regret.

STEP 7

Commit to God

"This is where your purpose is found."

Stop Running Away

Would you consider yourself a person who is afraid of commitment? If so, you are not alone. Millions of people throughout the world cringe at the very thought of making a commitment of any sort.

As a matter of fact, for many years, the very thought of committing myself to something would send me scrambling to get away. The reason for this is that I had always placed a great deal of value on freedom, and committing to something, to me, meant that I would be confined, restricted, and ultimately a prisoner to whatever type of commitment was made.

Inevitably, this fear of commitment had a tremendous impact on my life in regard to relationships, school, and the pursuit of various other goals. I would dabble here and there, try a little of this and that, but when the time came to give my word and make the commitment, I become extremely hesitant and would eventually find a way out.

Another area in which this fear of commitment existed was in my spiritual life. Although I believed in God and considered myself to be a Christian, I wasn't all in per se.

One reason for my reluctance in committing my life to God was the fear that if I were to make that commitment, I would be missing out on something. I always thought to myself, "Well, yes, I believe in God, but I can't commit myself to Him, I'm young, and I've still got a lot of living to do."

Ironically enough, what I didn't realize at the time was that my refusal to commit fully to God was the very thing that was keeping me from accomplishing my goals, as well as from the life that I truly wanted to live.

Commitment Will Lead to Your Happiest Life

Eventually, I began to come to terms with the fact that my fear of commitment was actually inhibiting my ability to live a full life. I realized that it was time to make a change.

One of the first major commitments that I made in my life was when I signed my name on the dotted line and joined the United States Air Force. It was a four-year commitment, and after fulfilling my military obligation and receiving an honorable discharge, I was proud of the fact that I had committed to something significant and fulfilled my end of the bargain. As a result of this commitment, my life as a young adult was heading in the right direction. I continued to carry this momentum in order to better my life, but in reality, I did not begin to make the life that I truly wanted a reality until I had committed myself to the Lord.

As human beings, an absolute truth that we must realize is that if we truly wish to attain a genuinely high level of fulfillment, happiness, and self-worth, we must commit ourselves to serving our

Heavenly Father and do our best to live our lives according to His will. As I've mentioned before, this notion may be intimidating to some, and that's okay. But you must realize that true happiness is impossible without committing your life to God.

As You Are Reading This, There's a Good Chance That You Are Missing Out

The fact of the matter is that many people today feel that if they were to commit their lives to God, they would be missing out on all the fun. They feel that once committed, there would be no more enjoyment in life. A common misconception is that all the things that we are told by today's society will bring us joy and fulfillment could no longer be a part of our lives if we truly committed ourselves to our Heavenly Father.

But it's important for us to realize that what many people consider to be fun may not be what is best for your life. For example, think for a minute of the multitude of commercials that you've seen trying to persuade consumers to purchase and consume alcohol. In these commercials, people are always having a blast. There's always some kind of goofy or quirky element involved that makes you laugh. Additionally, there is never any association that would make one associate anything negative with consuming alcohol.

In reality, consuming alcohol oftentimes lead to a lack of good judgment and self-control completely going out the window. Oftentimes conflicts get out of hand, with strangers as well as with people we know. Tragic events such as domestic abuse, assault, and driving accidents often occur. Relationships can suffer and sometimes end due to alcohol-related issues. The bottom line is that alcohol has the potential to destroy lives!

Alcohol commercials never show a person getting sick and vomiting in a trash can or arrests occurring while intoxicated, or even lives being destroyed by unnecessary car accidents.

The truth is that consuming alcohol normally starts out as something that is done in order to be social or to pass the time but oftentimes can lead to serious trouble. Nobody ever thinks that they could or would one day develop a problem or that it could have a negative effect on their life at some point down the road. Of course, if one could see into the future and see the oncoming complications in life created due to a lack of judgment, their choices concerning alcohol might be much different.

But every year, millions of people use and abuse alcohol, get arrested for driving while intoxicated, and some are injured and sometimes even tragically killed as a result of alcohol consumption.

Speaking from personal experience, I can honestly attest to the fact that nothing positive in my life ever resulted from the consumption of alcohol.

I'm certainly not suggesting that there are not people who are capable of drinking responsibly. I'm simply using this as an example of how marketers will try to manipulate consumers into believing that their product is a surefire way to make them happy, despite the fact that it may not.

Make God *the* Priority

Another important aspect of attaining true happiness in one's life is to make God *the* priority of your life. Notice that I use the word *the* and not *a* priority. The reason for this is because it is simply not good enough to make serving and glorifying your Heavenly Father a priority among your other top priorities, but rather God must take precedence over all other aspects of your life.

Once you make God your top priority above all else, you will soon realize that all other areas of your life will become what you've always desired them to be. In Matthew 6:33 (NIV), Jesus said, "Seek first His kingdom and His righteousness, and all these things well be given to you as well." What Jesus was trying to convey was that once you make God the priority of your life, everything else, including your family, finances, and literally every other facet of your life, will simply fall into place.

For years, I was guilty of making the mistake of neglecting to make God the priority in my life. My mind-set was that I was going to continue to live the way that I always had, trying desperately to find the right relationship, the right job, the right lifestyle, etc.

Despite my best efforts, no matter how hard I tried, things never seemed to line up. I was continually finding myself frustrated and depressed. I still possessed the notion that I wanted to improve my relationship with God, but I remember thinking to myself, "Once I get married and settle down, then I'll reconnect with my Heavenly Father."

What I didn't realize was that my rationalization at the time was the complete opposite of what it needed to be. I was blind to the fact that what I needed to do first was reconnect with my Heavenly Father, and then the rest of my desires for life would fall into place.

Lo and behold, once I made God *the* priority of my life, all the other goals that I had been pursuing but couldn't seem to attain began to manifest themselves, and life began to fall into place.

I firmly believe that in today's chaotic world, many people, perhaps even you, share the point of view that I had previously held. You are waiting until you get to a certain point in your life or attain a particular goal, and then you plan on committing yourself to your Heavenly Father.

But just as in my previous situation, you too may have your way of thinking backward. You see, your Heavenly Father loves you and wants nothing more than to have a relationship with you as His child.

And by neglecting to establish that bond, you are inadvertently preventing yourself from attaining all the gifts that God wants you to have.

No Pressure

I'm certainly not suggesting that if you commit your life to God, you can never make a mistake or slip up. I'm also not suggesting that you put a tremendous amount of pressure on yourself to be perfect. The Father knows that you and I are not perfect and never will be. There has only ever been one to have walked the earth who was perfect, and that was our Lord and Savior Jesus Christ. But what pleases our Heavenly Father is not whether or not we are perfect, but rather knowing that you are committed to Him and are putting your best foot forward in order to live a life that is aligned with His divine will.

Commitment Strengthens with Time

Your commitment to your faith, goals, and to being the best person that you can possibly be may not come easily at first, but you should begin by accepting Jesus Christ as your Lord and Savior. You should then establish how you intend on continuing and maintaining your commitment to God.

It may be something as simple as praying or meditating each morning, or it may be reading a few pages in your Bible each day. As you begin to move forward with honoring your newfound commitment to the Father, you will see that your discipline and your relationship with Him will continue to grow, and you will also become much more aware of His divine presence in your life.

As you continue to put effort toward making gradual, daily improvements and maintaining your commitment to growing in your relationship with God, it eventually will become a part of your normal daily life. You will also find that it will become easier to maintain. The positive habits that you develop will inevitably begin to have a positive impact on your entire life.

Consistency Is Key

By making a commitment and holding yourself accountable to uphold it, you will begin to develop consistency in your life. This consistency will ultimately result in positive changes and the type of life that you've always dreamed of.

As Olympic silver medalist and head wrestling coach at West Virginia University Sammie Henson simply puts it, "Consistency wins."

The Japanese call this philosophy *kaizen*. It is the notion that success and joy come from gradual, daily progress by holding yourself to your commitment and being consistent.

Regardless of what you call it, if you are willing to commit yourself to developing and maintaining these habits and making gradual continuous improvement, I promise you, it will not take long for you to begin to see significant improvement in the quality of your life.

It is not the notion of pursuing improvement in one's life or having a goal to accomplish that is difficult. Rather, it is having the discipline to maintain that consistency in the pursuit of a particular goal that determines whether or not one will become successful at accomplishing it.

Let's face the facts, any individual can pursue a goal or carry out the required steps to reach a particular goal for a short period of time. Whether it's exercising daily or waking up a few minutes early to put in some extra work, it doesn't take much effort to accomplish the task on a short-term basis.

But when the pursuit of that goal turns into days, weeks, months, and maybe even years, the person who can maintain their consistency in their pursuit will eventually experience success. The difficultly lies then in the discipline of holding oneself accountable and maintaining one's consistency in their pursuit.

Develop an Unwavering Resolve

Webster's Dictionary defines *resolve* as the following:

> *"1. To decide firmly on a course of action*
> *2. A firm determination to do something."*

If you are to live a life of true happiness and fulfillment, it is absolutely essential that you develop a deep resolve to uphold your commitment to the Father. When you develop unwavering resolve, you will always stay loyal to your faith and put your trust in God regardless of what challenges may arise.

Romans 5:3 states, "We also glory in our sufferings, because we know that suffering produces perseverance, perseverance character, and character hope."

As you continue to keep your commitment to God and stand by your godly principles throughout good times and bad, you will begin to see a dramatic increase in the strength of your faith, and you will discover a newfound sense of calm instilled in you each day.

You Can't Be a Fair-Weather Fan

Can you ever remember a time in your life when you've faced a challenge or hardship that led you to call on God's divine power to give you strength? What I'm referring to when I use the phrase "fair-weather fan" is a lack of consistency in the practice of one's faith.

Many people often try to utilize the "pick-and-choose" method when it comes to their faith and spirituality. What I mean by this is that for many, the only time that they go to God in prayer is in times of crisis. Oftentimes we are casually going through life, and suddenly we find ourselves faced with a challenge. For many, it is at these times that we find ourselves desperately seeking divine guidance and spiritual strength. This type of "selective servitude" is not the type of relationship that our Heavenly Father desires to have with us.

Anyone who is old enough to remember can tell you exactly where they were on the day of the horrific attacks on September 11, 2001. I remember seeing prayer vigils being held all over the nation, not only for those who had passed but also in support of those who had lost loved ones. American flags were flown everywhere in a display of solidarity. Our nation was unified as "Americans," and we put all our petty differences aside, supported one another, and collectively leaned on God to give us strength.

But unfortunately as the pain of the tragic event began to subside, many Americans began to revert back to their old ways. Petty squabbles began to reemerge, and for many, the sense of patriotism, compassion, and oneness as Americans began to dissipate, and most facets of society returned to pre-9/11 conditions. For many, God was put back on the shelf, and prayer was once again forgotten.

As is often the case when we face hard times in life, as the challenge passes, we find ourselves returning to the normalcy and comfort that we've become accustomed to, and our relationship with our Heavenly Father loses its precedence in our lives. We again become "lulled to sleep" by the comforts of life.

The Time Is Now

The simple truth is that God does not approve of this pick-and-choose type of obedience. Most times, God will not offer us a miracle if we only turn to Him in times of desperation. God desires our loyalty, obedience, and commitment to Him in good times and in bad.

We cannot be fair-weather fans of God and then in turn expect His favor and blessings to be present in our lives. On the other hand, if we commit ourselves to Him and continue to praise Him, serve Him, and walk in His ways, He will continue to offer blessings in ways and at a level that you cannot imagine.

Therefore, I implore you, don't look at your commitment to your Heavenly Father as a way of life that will require you to give something up or restrict your life in any way. Rather, look at your commitment as a way of living that will add stability, joy, pleasure, meaning, longevity, fulfillment, contentment, and overall happiness to your life.

He Wants You to Succeed

Have you ever wondered whether or not you were meant to enjoy happiness and success? Oftentimes we feel as though the world is against us in our pursuits, but nothing could be further from the truth. One thing that is important to note in your quest to create an amazing life is to remember that your Heavenly Father wants nothing more than for you to succeed. He will provide you with all the necessary resources and opportunities needed to accomplish your dreams, but only if you are willing to commit and live your life loving Him and dedicated to using your talents and abilities to glorify His name. Your Father desires a relationship with you, and just as any good parent wants to give their child an amazing life, He too wants only what's best for you.

Acknowledge His Blessings

Have you ever had an experience in your life that when looking back, you can't believe how things just seemed to fall into place? As you continue to strengthen your commitment to God, you will begin to experience a tremendous amount of good fortune and relative ease when pursuing your life's endeavors. This good luck comes not by chance or luck, but rather from your Heavenly Father.

Imagine offering someone that you love an immense gift, perhaps $100,000 or a brand-new car. Imagine if the individual to whom you had given the gift snatched the money or car keys from your hand without even an utterance of gratitude and simply drove away. If you are like most people, you would feel deeply insulted, perhaps even angry, and certainly hurt by their lack of courtesy to offer some sign of gratitude, and understandably so.

And yet this type of insult is exactly what our Heavenly Father endures each day from millions, perhaps even billions of people. The only difference is that the gifts that are offered by our Heavenly Father each day far surpass any amount of money or even the most expensive cars. Gifts such as an abundance of food, health, freedom, opportunities, guidance, and love are bestowed upon us, and yet some neglect to utter a simple word of gratitude for what their Creator has done for them.

When experiencing these blessings, it is essential that you acknowledge His goodness both in public and in prayer. The Father wants to know that you appreciate what He has done for you, and He will continue to shower you with His love and blessings for the rest of your life.

Count Your Blessings

The truth of the matter is that we have a tremendous number blessings in our lives for which we should be grateful. Many of us take so many things for granted, things that we may not even realize we have, such as our health or modern conveniences like electricity. We simply sometimes do not realize all that the Lord has done for us until something is taken away. A 2013 *Forbes* magazine article entitled "Astonishing Numbers: America's Poor Still Live Better Than Most Of The Rest Of Humanity" states that "the typical person in the bottom 5 percent of the American income distribution is still richer than *68 percent* of the world's inhabitants."

Another inspiring resource in regard to the improvements in the standard of living for virtually everyone in the world is the riveting 2010 book entitled *The Rational Optimist* by author Matt Ridley. In his book, Mr. Ridley does not just claim that "life is getting better—and at an accelerating rate," he goes on to offer a compelling explanation as to why the time period in which we are currently living is the best time period to have ever lived to date.

Mr. Ridley goes on to offer a vast amount of empirical data to support his theory and offers a convincing argument as to why our way of life today is of a far better quality than at any other time period. This argument pertains to virtually every aspect of life from the availability of food, access to clean water, vital resources, and medicine.

Mr. Ridley discusses goes on to discuss the notion of the world growing smaller and the profound impact that it has had on all our lives when he states,

> *"As I write this, it is nine o'clock in the morning. In the two hours since I got out of bed I have showered in water heated by North Sea gas, shaved*

*using an American razor running on electricity
made from British coal, eaten a slice of bread made
from French wheat, spread with New Zealand
butter and Spanish marmalade, then brewed a
cup of tea using leaves grown in Sri Lanka, dressed
myself in clothes of Indian cotton and Australian
wool, with shoes of Chinese leather and Malaysian
rubber, and read a newspaper made from Finnish
wood pulp and Chinese ink"* (Ridley 2010, 35).

He also goes on to discuss at length the vast improvements in the areas of communication, travel, mortality rate, and even addresses the level of comfort that each individual enjoys as opposed to a time not so long ago. Basically, Mr. Ridley's book is proof that throughout time, life has continually improved for virtually every country on earth, including those in the third world!

The point that I'm trying to make is that there is empirical evidence all around us that despite the fact that the world in which we live being far from perfect, we still have a tremendous amount of blessings that we should be grateful for. It is imperative that we recognize and acknowledge that!

Gratitude recenters us. It pulls us back into the right mind-set on a rough day. It reminds us that our Father in Heaven is still watching over us despite the challenges that we face in life.

The Grateful Leper

The book of Luke tells a story of ten lepers. As Jesus was on His way to Jerusalem, the men cried out, "Jesus, Master, have pity on us!"

Jesus, with the wave of a hand, cured all ten of the men. After the men had been healed, only a solitary man fell at Jesus's feet and offered him gratitude and praise for his miraculous healing. Jesus asked, "Were not all ten cleansed? Where are the other nine?" (Luke 17:11-17)

This story offers a picture that is not so different than what is often experienced today. Oftentimes we are suffering from one kind of difficulty or another. When we find ourselves facing hard times, we cry out to God in our prayers, begging for a solution to the problem. Then when the problem is remedied, we go about our lives as if the situation was overcome by mere chance. Just like the lepers in the story, once we are healed, we oftentimes forget to acknowledge what the Lord has done for us.

I cannot imagine a worse insult to our Father than to neglect to acknowledge the miracles that He has performed in our lives. You may be saying to yourself, "But I don't have anything to be thankful for." I promise you that there is a multitude of blessings for which you should be grateful. Just remember that no matter where you are in life, things could be worse and that your life is continually getting better.

The key to living the life of your dreams is to commit your life to your Heavenly Father, and when He continues to offer blessings in your life, be sure to acknowledge His divine goodness.

One of my favorite quotes by the renowned football coach Vince Lombardi states that "the quality of a person's life, is in direct proportion to their commitment of excellence, regardless of their chosen field of endeavor."

Therefore, I challenge you to commit to a life of excellence in serving your God. Regardless of what obstacles or challenges may arise, we cannot allow ourselves to be deterred from that commitment. I guarantee you that in a very short period of time after you make the commitment, you will begin to experience a tremendous amount of improvement in the quality of your life.

Commit to God

Regardless of the things that you have accomplished and the levels that you have or haven't reached, your life will never be complete, and your potential will never be fulfilled unless you follow through on step 7 and *commit to God*.

Embrace a Healthy Lifestyle

"This is where your vitality is found."

Ugh, It's Time to Get Up

Perhaps you have found yourself uttering these words to yourself more times than you would care to admit? A few years ago, a typical day in my life went something like this: At 5:30 a.m., my alarm would jolt me awake. My first thought normally had something to do with how exhausted I felt and how I couldn't wait to go back to bed later. This was followed by hitting the snooze button once or twice for a much-needed additional twenty minutes of sleep.

Eventually, after squeezing in every last second of sleep, I was forced to get up rather than be late for work. I would then peel myself out of bed and do my best to shake off the cobwebs by jumping in the shower.

As the morning progressed, the mental fog endured as I would then proceed to pour gallons of coffee down my throat in a desperate attempt to reach some sort of clarity. I always felt as though no matter how much sleep I had gotten, it wasn't enough. It seemed as though my day was spent in a mental fog, and on some days, even the most mundane of tasks felt too ambitious to even attempt.

After dragging myself through a long day, I would lie on the couch and drift off a bit before going to bed and doing it all over again the next day.

Perhaps this routine sounds familiar to you? Maybe your days tend to be even worse? If so, I have good news for you. You do not have to live the rest of your life in this lethargic, low-energy purgatory like so many others continue to do on a daily basis, year after miserable year. There is a way to escape this depressing lifestyle by making just a few simple but consistent changes.

What a Difference!

Now a typical day for me is drastically different. A normal day for me now goes something like this: My alarm goes off at 5:15 a.m., at which time I wake up feeling fully rejuvenated and refreshed. I begin my day thanking my Heavenly Father for the multitude of blessings that He has bestowed upon me. I continue this positive train of thought throughout the morning before heading off to work. My mind is clear, and my thoughts are lucid. My mood is great because I feel optimistic and energetic about the day. My interactions throughout the day are positive as a result of my mind-set. Performing necessary chores and errands after work is easy because my energy levels have been sustained throughout the entire day. I continue to stay productive through the evening hours until it is time to go to bed, at which time I sleep like a baby. My daily life has become so much more enjoyable and, overall, much happier.

The wonderful news is that you too can experience a similar transformation in your everyday life. There is simply no reason that you should live your life in a manner that is less than the absolute best.

Where's the Health?

Everywhere we turn in the United States Today, we see some element of health and the health industry. Whether it's the food labels promising "low fat" or "low sugar" on the multitude of products throughout every grocery store, the healthy items list at our favorite restaurant, or the never-ending list of commercials promising results if only we would try the latest nutritional plan or exercise equipment. Every day there are new gyms and fitness centers popping up in towns and cities across the nation. The fact of the matter is that we have become inundated with the idea of living a healthy lifestyle. It is no secret that the field of health and fitness has grown into a billion-dollar industry.

It seems very ironic then that with all the time, money, and resources spent toward improving our health and fitness, the obesity epidemic not only continues to grow but is actually gaining momentum. The rates of various lifestyle-related illnesses such as heart disease and diabetes continue to rise. According to the Heart Foundation, heart disease is the number 1 cause of death in America (http://www.theheartfoundation.org/heart-disease-facts/heart-disease-statistics/).

And it is not just our physical health that suffers from an unhealthy lifestyle. In my opinion, it is not a coincidence that a 2014 article on *cbs.com* reported that symptoms of depression in the United States are higher today than they were decades ago (http://www.cbsnews.com/news/americans-more-depressed-now-than-decades-ago/).

It seems as though while the nation continues to grow more and more physically unhealthy, the same can be said about its mental health.

With all the information, access, and resources dedicated to health, one would think that we should be living during the healthiest and happiest time in our nation's great history, but the very instinct that is designed to keep us alive, eating, is now the very thing that is killing us.

One simple fact that we must accept in our lives is that if we do not make a genuine, consistent effort to improve and maintain our health, we will never be happy.

Healthy Body = Healthy Mind

It is a simple fact of life: when you do not feel well, you are not happy. We've all had colds, the flu, and various other ailments, and it is no secret that we are usually in a miserable mood while our immune system battles "the bug." We struggle through the day tired, lethargic, and, overall, just feeling lousy. Complaining makes us feel better psychologically but does little to actually alleviate our suffering.

The truth of the matter is that the condition of our daily mood and temperament is no different whether we are sick from a temporary cold or flu, or sick from living an unhealthy lifestyle. When our bodies do not feel healthy, our energy levels are low, we feel lousy, and our bodies struggle to function efficiently. The result of this general feeling of poor health is an inevitable feeling of sadness.

It is absolutely necessary we realize that living a healthy lifestyle does not serve just the purpose of cosmetics or looking good. Of course, we would all love to shed a few pounds for beach season and feel confident walking around with a healthy physique, but the importance of being healthy is much greater than just wearing a bikini or showing off a six-pack. Your happiness, success, and overall livelihood literally depend on it.

I truly believe that the majority of health issues that millions of people suffer from on a daily basis including insomnia, lethargy, and poor digestion are all directly related to the amount of effort that one puts forth toward living healthy.

In turn, I believe that a tremendous amount of health issues could be alleviated and possibly even eliminated simply by making an effort toward living healthier.

If you aren't sleeping well, suffer from low energy levels, or experience other or even a combination of health issues, the simple fact is that you are not going to be capable of pursuing the life that you've always dreamed of living and, more importantly, the life that you deserve as long as you are forced to live with these conditions.

Whether you realize it or not, your poor health is affecting every facet of your life. The fact of the matter is that you simply cannot attain true happiness until you make a genuine, consistent effort to improve and maintain good health.

The Most Complex Machine Ever Made

I once had a wrestling coach in middle school who would oftentimes compare the human body to a high-performance race car. He would point out that it was essential to put the right "fuel" into our bodies in order to attain peak performance. He also said that failure to do so would result in low energy levels and ultimately poor performance.

This point was driven home to me when I was a teenager. I had mowed lawns all summer and was finally able to purchase a high-performance dirt bike. The problem with the bike was that if you wanted to just go out on the trail and "putt around," then this was not the bike for you. This bike was built to be run hard, and if you tried to take it easy while riding, it would literally break down and would require a number of repairs.

But when you took the bike out and ran it hard, it was second to none. From then on, when coach spoke of a high-performance machines and the correlation between the right fuel and its ability to be run hard, I knew exactly what he meant.

To this day, I love the analogy of comparing the human body to a high-performance machine, but I will take it a step further. Not only do our bodies react to the fuel that we put into them in the form of food and nutrition, but our bodies are far more complex than even the most sophisticated performance machines.

Your body is a machine, and it was designed to move and perform. Think for a minute of the ingenious design of our bodies and the way that we attain fuel by eating the foods that we need. Our bodies are designed to then extract the essential nutrients and convert it into fuel. Also, the way that we pull oxygen into our lungs, at which time it is transferred to our blood, which is then pumped and circulated throughout our body by the heart, is nothing short of amazing.

Many books have been written about the splendor of the human body, but oftentimes the miraculous efficiency and abilities of the body are taken for granted. It is important to realize that the human body functions much like a machine, in that it uses a variety of systems simultaneously in order to function. It is simply not enough to address one specific area of our health, but rather embrace our health as a whole. The truth of the matter is that our bodies function as one complex machine. As a matter of fact, it is the most complex machine that the world has ever known.

It is for this very reason that if one aspect of our health is suffering, it will inevitably affect other aspects of our health. And in turn, if we are healthy in one aspect, we will find that other facets of our health will be functioning properly as well.

For example, if our nutrition is suffering, we will experience low energy levels and perhaps digestive issues, and possibly even insomnia.

The same can be said regarding a lack of quality sleep. If you are unable to get a good night's sleep on a consistent basis, it will inevitably have an impact on how you feel. It's not just a matter of feeling tired, but also of difficulty functioning on a number of levels. The inability to think clearly, motivation levels, and even discipline in regard to nutritional needs can be affected when a person feels tired.

On the other hand, if we are maintaining a healthy lifestyle with proper nutrition, we will experience higher energy levels, smooth digestion, and a great quality of sleep.

Make Getting Healthy a Priority

Perhaps you are like millions of Americans who have tried to get healthy time and time again only to be left frustrated and disappointed? Perhaps you're one of the many who have tried various fad diets, weight loss pills, or fitness experiments or routines only to be left asking what went wrong? Maybe you feel that getting healthy, for you, is just not meant to happen and that it's just a case of poor genetics?

The truth of the matter is that despite the fact that different people can have different body types, everyone has the ability to get healthy. The reason that many people do not get healthy is because they fail to make getting healthy a priority. If you neglect to take this step, you will find that other elements of your life will take precedence over exercise and healthy eating habits. This, in turn, will lead you back on the guaranteed path to frustration and ultimate sadness. Getting and staying healthy should become a lifestyle rather than a temporary goal.

I once had a friend who, while at the gym one day, asked, "How do I get a six-pack?"

My initial response was, "Well, a big part of it is proper nutrition. The first thing you might want to do is give up alcohol for a couple of months."

Almost before I had gotten the words out of my mouth, he countered, "Well, I can't do that!"

It was at that point that I stopped offering advice because I realized the lack of commitment that my friend had to getting healthy. He was probably hoping to hear something easier, like "Drink lots of water."

But by making that comment without even giving any consideration to the idea, I realized that my friend lacked the resolve that it takes to get into the phenomenal shape that you see in movies and magazines.

The fact of the matter is that getting healthy is not and will not always be easy. You will have to work hard and even clean up your eating habits. But if you make being healthy a priority and visualize yourself as you want to be, healthy and happy, you will no doubt in time experience the positive benefits. The results of getting healthy will not only be beneficial physically but also psychologically. You will begin to experience positive changes in your mental state, including self-confidence. You will have higher energy levels in order to pursue goals, as well as better interactions and relationships with others. As you continue your healthy lifestyle, you will be able to carry this positive momentum with you for the rest of your life.

Utilize the KISS Principle

When it comes to diet and exercise, there is a tremendous amount of resources available. Unfortunately, due to conflicting information, data, and research, it has gotten to the point where most people are left confused. Many are not sure what they should or shouldn't eat or how they should or shouldn't exercise.

Many times, I have read an article written by a physician or expert pertaining to a particular diet that advocates eating a certain type of food, only to turn the page and find another article from a physician or expert advocating the complete opposite.

The same goes for training and exercise. Again, the media is riddled with conflicting articles and stories about the best way to train for maximum results.

This is not a book on diet and exercise, but being healthy is an essential component of being happy and maintaining a positive outlook on life. I would like to touch on a few important principles in regard to living a healthy lifestyle.

Also, I am not a certified nutritionist or physical trainer. I claim no expertise in these areas, but due to my athletic background and love of living healthy, I have spent a significant amount of time researching and experimenting with various types of nutritional and exercise plans.

As mentioned earlier, there is a tremendous amount of research available, and I encourage you to utilize some trial and error in determining which foods and exercises are best suited for you.

One reason that many people fail before they even attempt to get healthy is because of the overwhelming and contradictory information regarding getting healthy. Rather than trying to use overly complicated eating and exercise plans, I advocate simplifying your lifestyle and applying the KISS principle. *KISS* is an acronym that stands for *keep it simple, silly*.

It is my firm belief that by keeping your healthy lifestyle simple, you will be more likely to adhere to and maintain the healthy regimen that is best suited for you.

You Are What You Eat

First off, let's take a look at what one should eat. The main rule of thumb that you should implement in your nutrition plan is to do your best at eating only things that are found in nature. This would include everything from fruits, vegetables, lean meats, nuts, and, of course, a lot of water.

An example of an acceptable food would be fish. Obviously, fish are found in the natural world; therefore, fish would be a great component in a healthy nutrition plan. Another example would be broccoli. Again, broccoli is found naturally growing on the earth; therefore, it too is an excellent source of nutrition.

An example of what would not be good to eat would be crackers. Nowhere in the world could you go into a field and pick some fresh cheddar crackers. Therefore, they are not a good choice to include in your nutrition plan. Common sense and being honest with yourself are the best policies when it comes to determining food that should and should not be consumed.

Another important aspect of maintaining healthy nutrition is to ensure adequate water consumption. In the past, various sources would advocate drinking as much water as possible throughout the day. But in recent years, studies have shown that constant water consumption is not necessary and could actually be downright harmful. WebMD suggests between half an ounce to an ounce of water per pound of body weight, depending on the temperature and activity level. Basically, if you're thirsty, drink. Also, if your urine begins to turn a darker shade of yellow, you should probably increase your water intake. Water is essential for proper kidney function as well as flushing toxins from the body.

Many people try to substitute their hydration needs with diet sodas or other sugary drinks. Unfortunately, although they may taste good, many of these drinks do more harm than good. When it comes to hydration, whether before a workout, after, or throughout the day, nothing compares to good old quality H20.

You Must Eat!

One common misconception and disastrous mistake that often occurs when an individual is trying to get healthy and shed excess body fat, is that you must try to reduce your caloric intake as much as possible. But despite popular belief, nothing could be further from the truth.

As a matter of fact, although it may seem counterintuitive, one of the major reasons that people struggle when trying to lose excess body fat is that they are not eating enough. You see when you deprive your body of food, which is essentially the fuel that allows your body to run, your body begins to panic.

As mentioned earlier, our bodies are extremely complex, and when it senses that it is not receiving enough calories, it shifts into emergency reserve mode. In an ideal world, that would mean that it would begin to burn excess body fat in order to sustain our energy levels.

But in reality, what happens is our body begins to burn muscle in order to preserve the stored fat for when we are absolutely desperate for calories. The result is the "skinny-fat" look, which is the farthest thing from what anyone wants for their body.

It is imperative then that we continue to fuel our body with essential nutrients. Before you get too excited, this doesn't mean that you get to eat as much pizza and ice cream as you please, but instead that you need to continue fueling your body, approximately every two hours with smaller meals comprised of lean protein, as well as fruits and vegetables.

The Wrong Way to Lose Weight

During my competitive wrestling days, I was required to weigh a particular amount on the day of competition, commonly referred to as "making weight." If I would have been more intelligent about my methods to make the weight, I would have planned ahead, got on a quality nutritional program, and lost the weight gradually over a few weeks. At the time of the competition, I would have felt great, and my performance would have reflected how I felt.

I wish that would have been the case, but unfortunately, I must have been a glutton for punishment because most of the time, I would wait until the very last minute to lose the weight. Not only would I procrastinate in getting down to weight, but I would also try to find the easiest way to do it. This meant completely depriving myself of both solid foods and fluids. After a few days of eating literally one granola bar a day and restricting my fluid intake to almost nothing, I would normally make the weight. I would then proceed to eat and drink in excess following weigh-ins because I was completely dehydrated and starving. This resulted in feeling stuffed and bloated, and my performance suffered as a result.

As the season progressed, rather than trying to establish healthy eating habits that would allow me to maintain my competition weight, I would continue to use my unhealthy method of starvation and dehydration throughout the season. I was on a roller coaster of gaining and losing weight. The most detrimental aspect of this method of making weight was that as my body was trying to adapt to the fluctuations in my weight, it began to cannibalize the muscle from my body in an attempt to preserve my body fat for later.

By the end of the season, I had lost most of the hard-earned muscle that I had spent the entire off-season trying to develop. After months of physical and mental anguish, I was ready for the season to be over.

Had I better planned and been more disciplined, I believe that my success on the wrestling mat would have been much greater. But because I was not disciplined enough at the time, it was easier for me to starve myself rather than stick to a healthy nutritional plan that would have allowed me to make the weight, shed excess body fat, remain hydrated, and feel great.

The bottom line is that although most of us want to maintain a healthy weight in order to be a healthy individual rather than for competition, starving yourself is certainly not going to allow you to accomplish your goals.

You should allow yourself to eat and enjoy eating. It just takes a bit of discipline in order to hold yourself accountable when it comes to shedding excess body fat and feel the best that you possibly can.

Perception Is Reality

Another important component of being healthy is your *perception* of food. Many people see food as a source of pleasure. I remember a time in the past when every meal that I ate had to be absolutely delicious, and I always ate until I was ready to burst.

Food should not be seen as a source of pleasure, but rather as a way to provide fuel and nutrients to your body. After all, that is the reason that the Heavenly Father has provided us with food, so that we can nourish the body.

I'm not suggesting, however, that every meal has to be choked down with a look of disgust on your face. Part of the enjoyment of living healthy is finding new foods that are healthy and yet enjoyable to eat. And it's always fun to look forward to having a day where you can allow yourself to enjoy your favorite food, such as pizza or ice cream.

I promise you that if you begin to eat food that are full of nutrients and better for your body, you will feel a dramatic improvement in your mood and energy levels. Not only will your energy levels skyrocket and your mood improve, but you will be able to maintain those energy levels throughout the entire day, allowing you to pursue your goals. In turn, you will be able to live a life of fulfillment and happiness. In his famously popular *Poor Richard's Almanac*, Benjamin Franklin advocated these wise words, "Eat to live, do not live to eat." It would be in our best interest if we would follow Mr. Franklin's advice.

More Is Not Always Better

This rule tends to be difficult to grasp for some in our abundant society. We tend to look at all aspects of life as if a little is good, then a lot is not just better, but great!

But in most instances, that certainly is not the case. Two or three cups of coffee per day are probably fine and would provide much-needed antioxidants to the body. But when I see people carrying forty ounce coffee mugs out of the convenience store, it's time to call foul.

A great way to approach eating, and every other aspect of life for that matter, is to apply the Great Buddha's centuries' old adage of "all things in moderation."

Too much of anything is not good for you. A glass of milk will provide you with some great nutrients, but consuming an entire gallon in one day should probably be avoided.

As far as dairy products are concerned, there has been a considerable amount of literature as to whether or not we should consume these products. Again, I would approach these foods on an individual basis. Some individuals can consume dairy without a problem, whereas other individuals have difficulty with processing these foods. Therefore, play it by ear. If you find that dairy products aggravate your stomach or digestion, keep them to a minimum. However, if you feel fine after consuming dairy, then by all means feel free to consume them on a regular basis.

A Few Words on Training

As previously mentioned in regard to nutrition, there is also a tremendous amount of contradicting literature about to the proper way to train. And again, since this is not a book dedicated to exercise and training, I will just touch on a few basic guidelines so that you can utilize some trial and error to figure out what works best for your individual needs.

KISS Again for Training

Similar to what I had mentioned in regard to nutrition, it's easy to become overwhelmed with the tremendous amount of literature in regard to which way to train is best. As we all know, when the mind becomes overwhelmed, it oftentimes just wants to shut down. So along the same lines as nutrition, I advocate applying the KISS principle.

The truth of the matter is that if you truly desire to attain a life full of happiness, then proper nutrition isn't enough. To feel the best, most fulfilled, and happiest that you could possibly be, it is essential that you are implementing regular physical activity into your life as well.

Two of the most commonly asked questions in regard to training are "What type of exercises should I do?" and "how often should I do them?"

Basically, exercise is broken down into two categories; they are aerobic and anaerobic. The term *aerobic* means "with oxygen" and refers to exercise such as running, biking, and swimming. These types of exercise utilize oxygen for fuel. They can be done for longer periods of time, such as when you go for a jog or bike ride.

Aerobic exercise uses little or no resistance and is used to burn calories and improve cardiovascular health, which is of the utmost importance in today's world of obesity and heart disease.

The term *anaerobic* means "without oxygen" and refers to exercises such as lifting weights, pull-ups, or push-ups. These are exercises in which you are not burning oxygen for fuel, but rather the body's sugar or glucose supply. These exercises are more intense when performed and can last anywhere from a few seconds to a few minutes, such as in the case of doing a set of push-ups.

Anaerobic exercises are designed to strengthen muscles, ligaments, and bones. These exercises are essential as well in order to improve and maintain things such as mobility, bone density, and strong ligaments. Anaerobic training will also prevent muscle atrophy (loss of muscle) as we get older.

The most efficient way to improve overall health is to utilize what is known as cross-training. Cross-training means that you are combining both aerobic and anaerobic excises in the same workout. Exercises would include jumping jacks, rowing, or any exercise that would utilize some resistance performed at a higher intensity in order to increase your heart rate while simultaneously taxing your muscles.

There exists an ongoing debate as to which type of training is the best, but in my opinion, just as with nutrition, much of the type of training that you should do is based on the individual. Different individuals have different health goals. The important thing is that you get active, get your heart rate up, and get fresh oxygen pumping throughout your body.

Baby Steps

Your level of your current health should play a large role in deciding which exercises you should initially start with. Remember, safety first. If you have been inactive for a number of years, it would probably not be a great idea to try running five miles on your first day out. Rather, maybe you should start out with walking, then as you continue to improve, you may want to increase your pace and/or distance.

The same applies to all other exercise as well. Set reasonable goals for yourself, and as those goals are reached, continue to set new ones.

Have Fun with It

One aspect of training that you should take into consideration is to choose activities that you enjoy. If you enjoy getting out into nature for a walk or jog, then by all means, do it. If you're an individual that enjoys lifting weights, then lift weights. You should always utilize the option of switching things up, changing your routine, or trying something new. As your health continues to improve, you may find yourself becoming more confident, which may lead to experimenting with new types of workouts that you've never done before.

It is important to be careful not to force yourself to do exercises that you simply despise. There is no faster way to sabotage yourself in your pursuit of getting healthy than to force yourself to embark on activities that you hate. In turn, you will look for every excuse to skip your workout. Although exercise is not always seen as something that is done for enjoyment, it's all about perspective. You shouldn't view training as grueling, miserable work. Remember, this is another step to becoming the best and happiest that you can possibly be. Maintain a positive perspective.

Stay Loose

One last area that I would like to address, due to the fact that it is highly neglected in Western culture, is the importance of stretching.

Stretching is often seen as an afterthought and something that most people, especially Americans, treat as an expendable part of one's healthy lifestyle. But nothing could be further from the truth.

Many Asian cultures have embraced the importance of stretching for centuries, which is evident in the widespread practice of yoga in India and tai chi in China. And despite the recent surge of popularity of yoga in the United States, most people in Western society still have not fully embraced the practice of stretching. But as we grow older, our bodies become more and more stiff, we lose the dexterity in our muscles, and our ligaments become tight and nonpliable.

Think of yourself when you were young. The odds are that you were much more flexible, much more active, and rarely got sore, even after a hard day of playing outside. But as you've grown older, you've become stiffer and find it harder to recover from a strenuous workout or maybe even just going about normal daily activities, such as a stressful day of work.

As our bodies age, we become naturally tighter. But just as with our strength and cardiovascular conditioning, with a continual stretching routine, it is possible to improve, maintain, or even regain your flexibility for the rest of your life no matter what your age.

Ouch! Our Aching Backs

According to the American Association of Neurological Surgeons, 75–85 percent of all Americans will experience some form of back pain in their lifetime (http://www.aans.org/. Low Back Pain. May 2016). Unfortunately for many, the pain becomes chronic and long-term. Many seek relief for their pain by either taking pain medication or enduring invasive surgery. But more times than not, these remedies are only a temporary fix, and the back pain continues to persist.

Most people neglect to realize that back pain is often caused by a lack of flexibility and tightness in the hamstrings, which can be easily remedied with a continual, consistent stretching routine.

It's no secret that people oftentimes tend to carry a tremendous amount of stress and tension in their muscles. Most people do not realize this, but it manifests itself oftentimes physically through headaches, high blood pressure, and difficulty relaxing and unwinding.

I'm not trying to sell you a product or system of stretching, but I am simply stating that you cannot afford to neglect this aspect of your health any longer. There is a substantial amount of resources available on different types of stretching ranging from DVDs, online videos, books, as well as classes with certified instructors available at most gyms.

Whether or not time constraints keep you from attending yoga classes, it is still imperative to your overall health and happiness to develop a good stretching routine. A brief ten-minute morning and evening stretch will make a world of difference in your energy levels, as well as in the amount of stress and tension that you carry around on a daily basis. Within a few short weeks, you will feel more limber, lighter, younger, more energetic, and, overall, happier with your newfound flexibility.

Sleep Like a Baby

According to National Public Radio.org (NPA.org), insomnia affects roughly sixty million Americans. And although it is widespread, scientists disagree on the best way to treat it. Many people seek relief through the aid of prescription and over-the-counter sleep aids. In reality, the problem that most people deal with in regard to sleep and insomnia could be remedied by simply getting active. By utilizing regular exercise and stretching, many people would see their sleeping difficulties disappear.

Oftentimes people leave work and feel absolutely exhausted, but it's important to realize that the tiredness that is felt by most people is actually mental and emotional fatigue. At these times, exercise would actually make the individual feel more energized and relaxed at the same time.

Have you ever gotten home from work feeling absolutely spent despite having had very little physical activity throughout the day? Teaching, as with many jobs, is a very emotionally taxing career. I can remember many times after a stressful, hectic day coming home and thinking that the last thing that I felt like doing was getting in a workout. Rather than exercise, people oftentimes turn to another source of comfort such as food or television. Unfortunately, this can become a habit that inevitably leads to an even greater feeling of lethargy and weight gain. It's no secret that oftentimes the amount of stress that an individual has been experiencing is revealed by the effect that it has on their appearance. It is for this very reason that the nineteenth-century philosopher James Allen once stated, "The outer conditions of a person's life will always be found to reflect their inner beliefs."

Failure to find a healthy outlet for stress is one of the most detrimental mistakes that a person can make in their pursuit of happiness.

When I found myself feeling fatigued and stressed, I would remind myself that the exhaustion that I was feeling wasn't physical but rather mental and that I would actually feel energized and refreshed by doing some exercise. Looking back, I cannot remember a single time that after working out after a stressful day that I wished that I hadn't. Rather, every time after working out, I realized that it was exactly what I had needed.

Improve Your Health, Improve Your Life

Despite what some readers may think, embracing a healthy lifestyle is as important to attaining a happy life as any other step in this book.

By embracing a life of healthy nutrition and activity, you will not only see an improvement in your physical appearance and energy levels, but you will also feel an improvement in your mental and spiritual health as well. Whether you experience difficulties in your digestion, quality of sleep, your mental clarity, or some other aspect of your life, I promise that you will find that once you address one aspect of your health, you will see progress in all other aspects as well.

Again, I'm not advocating any particular product or system, but rather that you focus on getting healthy. The important thing is to get started and keep your momentum moving in a positive direction. I guarantee that it won't take long before you notice the tiredness evaporating and your energy levels skyrocketing, and a newfound positive feeling and mind-set will emerge that will allow you to live a long, happy life.

Embrace a Healthy Lifestyle

Stop allowing the feelings of exhaustion and lethargy keep you from the happiness that life has to offer. By making a few simple adjustments and deciding to *embrace a healthy lifestyle*, you will inevitably begin to feel not only healthier, but happier in your daily life.

STEP 9

Cultivate Patience

"This is where your enjoyment is found."

I Feel the Need for Speed

Have you ever found yourself saying, "I wish this thing could go faster?" Or perhaps, "Why is this taking so long?" If so, you are not alone. It is no secret that we live in a fast-paced, high-speed, on-the-go society. We have grown accustomed to the various events of our day occurring in the blink of an eye. Innovations in the field of transportation, food, communications, and literally every other aspect of our lives have created a society that moves at a blinding pace.

And with the advent of the Internet and social media, literally every facet of society is being streamed and updated with every passing second. We are fully aware of the events unfolding not only in our own small corner of the world but in every other corner of the world as well. As time continues to progress, things certainly do not seem to be slowing down, and chances are, they never will.

But along with technological progress comes a downside. The price that must be paid for this societal acceleration is that many people today are losing their ability to be patient. The severity of our impatience has increased gradually, which causes a lack of awareness in regard to its occurrence, but it is happening nonetheless.

If you're not convinced of this notion, I'll offer you a simple example. Imagine going back in time to the "good ol' days" of dial-up Internet. Now that we've all become accustomed to our high-speed Internet service, in which the Web page appears at the click of a button, we would surely loose our cool (and our minds, for that matter) if we had to wait more than thirty seconds for our Web page to appear (not to mention if we were forced to endure that nails-on-a-chalkboard sound that we used to hear every time that we connected to the Internet).

It's difficult for us today to imagine what life would be like if we were forced to return to the "slow-paced" world that existed not so long ago.

Imagine growing up with high-speed Internet as young people do today. You simply could not fathom being forced to wait minutes for a Web page to load.

Travel itself was a rarity for many in the early years of our nation due to its arduous nature. No elaborate road or highway systems had been established, and travel was done mostly on foot, horseback, or by carriage ride. Many today travel further in one direction for work than some would travel in a lifetime in the decades not so long ago.

And what about the rate of speed at which we've become accustomed to traveling in our vehicles each day? The first mass-produced car, the Ford Model T, traveled at only forty miles per hour. If you were traveling on the highway today at 40 mph, you'd be getting more than a few odd looks and could possibly even cause an accident.

Those of us who have been on the planet longer than some can remember a time when we were not in constant correspondence with every person in our lives at all times throughout the day. Or when the dreaded time came to work on a research paper, we actually had to travel to a library and utilize the Dewey Decimal System in order to complete our work.

The point that I'm trying to make is that in this ever-increasing fast-paced world that we live in, the majority of us have lost our ability to be patient. Others have never had it at all.

Some may ask, "Well, why should I be patient? After all, I have places to go, people to see, and things to do." This is no doubt true, but the fact of the matter is that your lack of patience could very well be the thing that is keeping you from attaining not only the goals that you've set for yourself but also the happiness that you desire for your life.

We Are *Not* Born Patient

Patience, you see, is a learned skill that needs to be developed and cultivated through awareness and conscious effort. I'm quite certain that for most people, the ability to be patient is not an innate skill.

In the past, human beings were not necessarily patient by choice. Rather, patience was something that was acquired (or maybe I should say required) most likely because those who lived in the past had no other choice. A lack of technology in communication and transportation left those who lived not so long ago with no other option but to wait patiently while taking a carriage ride to another city. They were forced to wait days, weeks, or even months for a response to a correspondence.

As a historian and social scientist, I oftentimes analyze in wonder the impact that modern technology has had on our society. I also speculate as to how history may have changed had certain advancements come sooner. For example, the deadliest battle of the War of 1812 was tragically fought after a treaty had already been signed.

Unfortunately for those who fought, news of the treaty did not reach the United States until almost a month later.

The fact that it is possible to carry on a "real-time" conversation with virtually anyone in the world or travel great distances in short periods of time has caused us to become disconnected with our ability to be patient.

I'm certainly not suggesting that we all haven't benefitted tremendously from the advent of technology. Many facets of life have improved through the ability to share and acquire significant amounts of information, as well as the ability to access various resources quickly and easily.

But being an individual who has had the opportunity to have experienced the earlier years of my life (through high school) before the Information Age, and then having had a career in education after the Technological Revolution, I feel as though I've had a front-row seat and witnessed both the benefits and pitfalls of technology's impact on society.

And as I have adapted to a faster-paced world, I have found myself losing the ability to be patient as well. I realized that when it came to moments where patience was required, such as standing in line at the grocery store or sitting at a red light, I was becoming more and more agitated. It is completely normal to find ourselves becoming impatient from time to time. The important thing regarding this issue is to become aware of our lack of patience and then conscientiously work to improve ourselves in that particular area.

Perhaps some may wonder, "What's wrong with wanting things to occur faster? Isn't that what progress is about? Shouldn't we find faster, more efficient ways to get things done?" My answer to those questions is absolutely—to a certain extent.

You see, most of us have become so accustomed to every need or desire being fulfilled instantaneously that if it doesn't happen as quickly as we would like, we become frustrated. Whether it be getting fast-food or downloading our favorite song, it all happens in the blink of an eye.

The problem lies in the fact that the brain does not have a simple on and off switch that we can flip that allows us to be patient at times when it is required and be more "on the go" at others. This has caused us to become hard-wired for instant gratification. When we want something, we want it now. We don't want to wait, even for a minute.

True Happiness Requires Patience

The greatest detriment associated with a lack of patience comes at times when we are trying to achieve our more meaningful goals. As we all know, oftentimes the things in life that come easily are not the most important. For example, doing the bare minimum to simply earn a passing grade in high school or college requires relatively little effort. On the other hand, earning an A+ or perhaps making the honor roll or dean's list will require a substantial amount of studying and effort.

When it comes to achieving meaningful goals in life such as starting a business from scratch or getting in phenomenal physical condition, we no longer have the patience to see these goals through. We have become so accustomed to things happening in an instant that when they don't, we simply give up or abandon the goal altogether.

One of the key ingredients to creating the life that we desire and finding ultimate happiness is the cultivation of patience. The reality of the fact lies in the notion that the more lofty the goal, the more time and effort we must be willing to dedicate to the pursuit of it. If one is lacking in the area of patience, they will limit themselves to only achieving the goals in life that are more superficial and easier to attain.

Trust God's Timing

Just as any good parent would attest, you don't give a child whatever they want on a whim. Giving a child their every desire at a moment's notice results in creating a spoiled child that, in turn, becomes a spoiled adult.

Although oftentimes children do not see the big picture when a parent refuses to buy them a new toy, or a new car for that matter, when they become more mature, they will look back and realize the valuable life lessons that the parent was trying to instill in them by not giving in to their every desire. The parent is well aware of the importance of instilling values, such as fiscal responsibility, that will ultimately benefit the child for the rest of his or her life.

Oftentimes parents will set up a system of chores and payment in the form of allowance in order to teach their child the importance of working hard and earning that which you desire in this world. Children who are taught these kinds of lessons are very grateful when they reach adulthood and realize the tremendous benefit to their life as a result.

Our Divine Father watching over us from heaven is no different. In His infinite wisdom, He knows that we would learn absolutely nothing about life by giving in to our every desire like a spoiled child.

If our Heavenly Father gave in to our every desire in the blink of an eye like some sort of genie in a bottle, the end result would be a world of absolute chaos. And just as we love our children more than we can put into words, our Creator loves us infinitely more.

Just as any parent would attest, they would love nothing more in the world than to give their child their every desire, due to the fact that they want to make them happy. But parents restrain themselves in their effort to teach their child morals and values. It would do them a tremendous disservice to spoil them. Our Heavenly Father is in a similar position. He knows that despite His love, He cannot allow Himself to spoil us.

Regardless of how we may feel personally and how frustrated we may become because things may not be happening as quickly as we would like, it is imperative to remember that our Heavenly Father knows what is best for our lives. He may be willing to open a door of opportunity in our lives, but not until the time is right. In the Book of Ecclesiastes King Solomon speaks of the importance of acknowledging that there is a season for everything in life. Therefore, it is of the utmost importance to remember that no matter what we are pursuing, whether it be finding a partner or trying to have a child, God's timing is perfect. Our dreams will be fulfilled when the time is right. (Ecclesiastes 3:1-8)

Some may say to themselves, "I've been waiting for this blessing to unfold for years. Why is God forcing me to wait so long?" It is important to remember that although we may want something that we believe is in our best interest, our Father may know something that we may not. Perhaps it is not what would be best for our lives, and therefore it will never happen regardless of how long we wait.

If you are pursuing a goal or dream for an extended period of time and it seems as though there is no progress being made, it is in your best interest to take a step back and reevaluate the situation in an honest manner. Perhaps it's a relationship with a spouse or significant other that has been struggling. You wish more than anything that the two or you could sort things out. Sometimes it just seems from our biased perspective that if we could just have them back or somehow fix that mistake, all would be well in the world. Unfortunately, this simply is not always the case. There are times in our lives where we must accept the fact that this person or dream is not what is best for our lives or is not supposed to come to fruition for reasons that do not become evident until further down the road. There is a tremendous amount of truth in the old adage that "hindsight is 20/20."

Oftentimes we don't see the big picture until long after events have had a chance to play themselves out, and many times when they do, we look back with a smile and say to ourselves, "Wow, I'm sure glad that didn't work out!" This may seem counterintuitive. But there will certainly be times in your life when it seems that things did not go your way, only for you to look back weeks, months, or even years later and realize that things not working out as planned truly was the best thing that could have happened and has actually worked out in your favor.

Listen to Your Heart

We've all been told at some point in our lives to listen to our heart. Most often when I've been told this, I wrote it off as something people would say when they were uncertain of what else to say. But this is advice that all of us would do well to follow.

If we would trust our intuition, we would find that going with our gut is more oftentimes than not the right way to go. The reason for this is because when you listen to your heart, it is actually your Heavenly Father speaking in a way that you are not consciously aware of. Oftentimes God tries to direct our paths by speaking to us deep down inside.

Many times when making an important decision in life, we initially feel a strong sense of which direction we should go, only to go on to struggle with making the decision. This is due to the fact that rather than go with our initial feeling, which is God speaking to us, we allow our conscious mind to interfere.

Some may be wondering, "When will I know to be patient or if I should let go?" A number of years ago, I came up with a phrase for when I found myself stressed about making a decision. I would simply say to myself, "If it is His will, it will be." This would reinforce the notion in my mind to put the situation in God's hands and let Him decide the outcome. Throughout the years, I have found myself saying this quite often and have found the outcome to always be what was best.

God Will Test Your Faith

It has been said that adversity is not a case of *if*, but rather *when*. We need to keep this in mind when facing challenges in life. Our Heavenly Father will test our faith and resolve in order to see how badly we truly wish to achieve whatever it is that we are striving toward. It is important that in these difficult times that we trust in our God and continue to forge ahead toward our goals and a better life. When you find yourself in a situation in which you're left wondering whether or not you should continue to wait for your goal to come to fruition, you simply need to find a quiet place to pray. Simply ask your Heavenly Father to offer you guidance in knowing what is best for your life. I promise you that although it may not seem as though the answer comes to you instantly, God will speak to your heart, offer you guidance, and allow you to know which direction you should go. I promise you that if you trust in God and continue to put your best foot forward, if it is in your best interest, no matter what the goal, it will come to fruition.

In the book of Matthew, Jesus states, "If you believe, you will receive whatever you ask for in prayer." (Matthew 21:22) It is important for you to realize that whatever you ask for in prayer, God will fulfill on two conditions. The first is that you are asking with a pure heart full of faith and without doubt in your mind. The second stipulation is that God will give you whatever it is that you ask for *if* it is what is best for your life. If these conditions are met, then there is nothing that God will not give you in this life. But we must trust in His divine wisdom. Unfortunately, there may be times when you ask God for something in prayer, but you do not receive it. In this instance, it is important take a step back and remind yourself that He knows what is best for your life.

When striving toward a goal, be sure to stay strong in your faith. Jesus once stated, "With God *all* things are possible." (Matthew 19:26) Notice He did not say *some* things are possible or *most* things are possible, but rather that *all* things are possible. Do not be limited in your faith by your limited mind. Believe that God will answer your prayers, and it will be so.

Emotions Run High

Dick Vermeil is one of the most successful and well-respected men to have ever coached in the National Football League. Coach Vermeil's career spanned the better part of four decades, yet he actively coached only fourteen seasons of those forty years.

If you're not familiar with Coach Vermeil's story, you may be wondering why a man who is known as being one of the hardest working, most likeable, most inspirational figures to have graced the sport and was named Coach of the Year at four different levels only coached fourteen out of forty years?

You see, Coach Vermeil is an extremely passionate man. He wears his emotions on his sleeve and has been described by his players as a man who isn't afraid to let people know how he feels. And although the passion and emotion that Coach Vermeil had put into his career was most certainly one of the keys to his success, it was also the reason that he had to take a fifteen-year hiatus from coaching after spending four years with the Philadelphia Eagles. When the fire inside burns so intense, it can lead to great success, but unfortunately it can also take a toll on a person mentally and may even lead to emotional burnout.

Coach Vermeil describes a day when he arrived at the stadium for practice, and he simply could not get out of his car. He wasn't sure why. He was forced to call his wife and ask her to come and pick him up. It seems as though Coach Vermeil had gotten to a point where after committing himself so completely to his trade, he could simply go no further (*A Football Life* 2015).

Coach Vermeil decided that it was best for him to step away from coaching for a while in order to take a break and rejuvenate. He spent the next decade and a half in broadcasting, learning and evolving in his perspective on coaching and on the game in general.

After over a decade away from coaching, Coach Vermeil felt the competitive fire burning once again and decided that it was time to return to coaching. Not only did he return, but he did so in a very triumphant manner. As a matter of fact, he would go on to lead the St. Louis Rams to an exciting victory in Super Bowl XXXIV.

An important aspect of Coach Vermeil's career that we need to realize is that although he enjoyed tremendous success in the latter part of his career, it was necessary for him to step away from the game for a while and take some time to rejuvenate emotionally so that he could perform optimally as a coach.

Coach Vermeil's story serves as an example not only for how important it is to allow yourself time to rejuvenate emotionally to be happy but also for how it is never too late to finish something that you have started.

If there is a goal or endeavor in which you may have given up on or fallen short of achieving, it is never too late to go back and finish the job.

Take Time to Rejuvenate

Many of us today find ourselves in a similar situation as Coach Vermeil. Although we may not be coaching at the highest level in the NFL, we are living stressful, hectic lives that can wear us down emotionally nonetheless.

And because we are all human beings and we all have an emotional breaking point, it is vitally important that we take the time to step back, rejuvenate, and refocus before returning to the grind. The time needed varies from person to person. You may only need a few minutes, whereas others may need a few days, a few months, or in Coach Vermeil's case, a few years.

An important thing to remember is that if we remain mindful and careful not to push ourselves to our absolute breaking point, most times it will not take as long to recover.

Learn to Relax

Just as I had mentioned earlier, patience is something that needs to be learned and cultivated rather than something that we are innately born with. At the same time, the same can be said for one's ability to relax. Oftentimes people find themselves in a situation where they've become so accustomed to being on the go and constantly busy for such a prolonged period of time that they simply aren't quite sure how to relax.

The truth of the matter is that many of us have been going at full speed in order to meet and maintain the demands of our lives that when things come to a screeching halt and we get a chance to breathe, we're not quite sure what to do. Oftentimes when people find themselves in this situation, rather than taking some time to really relax and rejuvenate, they find something else to keep themselves busy, such as meeting friends out for a drink or distracting themselves with social media or television.

Perhaps you have found yourself in this situation? Has there ever been a time when you've reached the end of the weekend only to feel more exhausted than you were at the end of the workweek? Or maybe you've gone on vacation to get away from things for a while, only to find that upon returning home you have a feeling of depletion and need a vacation from your vacation? In our high-paced world, many of us feel as though if we get a few minutes or even a few days out of work, we need to fill every second with some sort of activity.

Even the Creator of the universe needed a day to rest, and He knew that it was vital to our happiness and well-being that we too should have time to rest and rejuvenate at the end of a busy week. Unfortunately many people find that they are actually busier on the weekend than they are during the week.

The truth of the matter is that just because you are not at work or running errands doesn't mean that you are relaxing. And with the advent of technology, many people find themselves spending their free time caught up with catching up on the latest happenings of friends and family, which can literally be exhausting in itself.

Rather, what we should do when trying to relax and rejuvenate is give ourselves a chance to disconnect from it all. That means turning off the television and the phone and allowing oneself to quiet their mind. Find somewhere quiet to go and meditate, or perhaps go for a nice walk in nature and do some active mediation. Fresh air can work wonders for a person that has been cooped up all week in an office or in the house.

Allow yourself time to decompress and not worry about completing your to-do list. Put your worries on hold. And remember, there is absolutely nothing wrong with putting off returning calls or running errands for a few hours when you feel the need to rejuvenate your mind and body.

It's a good idea to personalize your relaxation methods. You can also try varying your methods in order to accommodate the weather and time constraints. You may just need a few minutes to close your eyes at your desk and visualize yourself at your favorite beach or relaxing location. Other days you may want to drive to the park and go for a walk. You don't have to leave your phone in the car for safety reasons, but discipline yourself to wait until you finish your walk or activity before you return any calls or texts. Take this time to be alone with your thoughts.

Focus on Your Blessings

When you find yourself feeling stressed out, it is a perfect time to take a minute and remember all the blessings for which you are grateful for in life.

Oftentimes when work starts to pile up or we find ourselves asking why it is that we have to deal with stress and challenges, it always serves as a great relief to step back and focus on all the blessings that your Heavenly Father has bestowed upon you.

Whether it be your health, your family, or simply the food on the table and the roof over your head, when we take time to stop and thank God for what He has done for us in our lives, it always brings one back to reality and restores focus and creates a positive state of mind. You can do this throughout the day. Remembering your blessings tends to keep things in perspective.

Why the Rush

Would you say that you're the type of person that is always in a hurry? Do you get angry when stuck behind a slow-moving car or when your Internet connection is at a crawl? Simple inconveniences such as these can add to our already overflowing level of stress throughout the day.

Despite those times when you are on a tight schedule, whether it's to pick the kids up from school or to make it to your doctor's appointment on time, there really is no need to feel stressed when things take a few more minutes than expected. Many times we find ourselves with a laundry list of items that we need to accomplish throughout the day, but the truth of the matter is that if we get caught in construction that sets us back five, or even twenty minutes, it really isn't the end of the world.

Other than being an annoyance, most times those extra few minutes are nothing more than a minor inconvenience. If you arrive home a few minutes late or are running a few minutes behind to meet your friend for lunch, it's important to not allow yourself to get angry about the situation. Simply say to yourself, "I guess this isn't *that* big of a deal," keep a smile on your face, and all will be well.

Simplify Your Life

Another source of stress for many today is a tendency to overcompli-cate things. What I mean by this is that what has emerged in today's society is an expectation that every event, whether it be a birthday party or a proposal to senior prom, must be planned out and exe-cuted with the utmost complexity and showmanship.

We've all seen on television the elaborate birthday parties that are thrown for adolescents turning sixteen or the ever-increasing complex ways in which "promposals" are carried out. I firmly believe that in today's increasingly small world, which is interconnected through technology, keeping up with the Joneses has become more difficult than ever.

The result is more stress on individuals both financially and psychologically. Parents are expected to spend insurmountable amounts of money because they want their child to enjoy the same experiences as those who are far better off financially. This, in turn, leads to an increase in stress, which affects virtually every aspect of their life.

Many people, in their undying love for their friends and family, have continued to increase the number of hours spent at work in order to make more money and still find themselves with huge amounts of debt due to their attempt to provide whatever item or experience that they feel is important to their loved ones. The effects of this in the long run can be detrimental to one's health and relationships.

The best way to counter this is to simplify your life. What I mean by this is that rather than planning a birthday party with all the extravagance of a royal wedding, invite some friends over, order a few pizzas, put some good music on the stereo, and just enjoy one another's company. After all, what is the experience about, how much money was spent or enjoying laughs and spending quality time with a close group of friends and family?

Complex Does Not Equal Better

A few years ago, a friend of mine bought a new car. My friend loved this car. It included all the bells and whistles imaginable. It was a beautiful shade of royal blue, had a backup camera, heated seats, a DVD player for the kids, and even a sensor that allowed you to put your foot under the back bumper to open the hatch for those times when your arms were full of groceries.

It was an extravagant vehicle, and my friend was ecstatic to own it. He couldn't say enough about how great this vehicle was. He mentioned it at every opportunity. But after a couple of months, my friend began to reassess the fact that perhaps his new car wasn't as amazing as it had initially seemed.

A few months after my friend had purchased his car, he stopped by for a visit. To my surprise, he pulled in driving a different car. I asked him if he had traded in his beloved blue vehicle. He said no, but rather it had had a malfunction that needed to be fixed and was at the shop. The car that he was driving was a loaner, but he was supposed to have his prized vehicle back in about a week or so.

A few months later, my friend and I had gotten together to grab lunch, and again this time he was driving a different vehicle than the time before. Again I inquired into whether he still had the car that he had purchased a year or so before. Again he replied with a sigh, stating that his vehicle was in the shop, this time due to a different malfunction. And in fact, this had actually been the fourth or fifth time that the car had been in the shop in the past year. My friend even went on to say that he and his wife had been considering looking for a new vehicle.

I was somewhat surprised due to the fact that he had been so elated at the purchase of the vehicle, with all its marvelous features, and was now thinking of finding something new to drive. But I quickly came to the realization that it wasn't the vehicle itself that my friend wanted to get rid of, but rather all the problems that the vehicle had.

The point that I'm trying to make is that despite what our mind may assume in regard to the complexity of something, whether it be a vehicle or a get-together, bigger and more elaborate may not necessarily be better. As a matter of fact, it actually opens up the possibility of more things to go wrong.

My friend loved his vehicle, and it was great, but there were so many electronics included and features that could potentially malfunction that it was virtually inevitable that it would break down in one way or another.

On the other hand, I once owned an older vehicle that was very basic, for lack of a better term. It had manual windows and very few conveniences that are considered to be absolutely essential in today's vehicles. And yet I drove that vehicle for the better part of a decade with very few issues in regard to maintenance other than normal wear and tear. As a matter of fact, I was able to get over two hundred thousand miles on the vehicle, and when I decided to upgrade, it was still a strong running vehicle, and even better yet, I was able to sell the vehicle for almost what I had paid for it.

Although it may seem counterintuitive to most of us, oftentimes the simpler something is, the better. We should apply this philosophy to our lives as well.

If you work to simplify your life, I believe that you will find that your stress levels will be lower, and you will actually find more pleasure and happiness in the peace of mind that comes from not trying to manage all the things that can or possibly will go wrong.

Just Breathe

Although most of us do not have hours each day to spare, and sometimes feel as though we can't even get a minute of downtime, it is imperative that we find time throughout the day to allow ourselves to decompress.

An important aspect to decompressing is to be aware of our breathing. Whether we're talking about the Navy SEALs, top-level elite athletes, or yoga practitioners, the importance of breathing has emerged at the forefront of many training regimens and remains a priority when it comes to focus and relaxation. The truth of the matter is that many people go throughout their day stressed out and tense. In turn, their breathing unknowingly becomes very shallow. The result is poor oxygen flow throughout the body and a feeling of low energy or even fatigue.

According to yoga therapist Kate Holcombe of YogaJournal. com, proper breathing can "treat people with a variety of issues including depression, anxiety, sleep disturbances, chronic pain, and even life-threatening illness" (Holcombe 2012)

Former Navy Seal and founder of SEALFIT, Mark Divine, has written extensively on the importance of breathing for Navy SEALs on high-level missions, as well as the average person simply looking to improve their level of fitness.

Whether you're an athlete trying to get through a tough workout or a mother who is trying to relax on a stressful day, Mark recommends a technique that he calls "box breathing."

As discussed on Mark's website sealfit.com, box breathing basically refers to breathing using a square box pattern with each side lasting for a count of five.

According to sealfit.com, box breathing can be used to treat "long-term anxiety reduction, chronic pain relief," as well as "to create an increased sense of well-being," along with a list of other benefits (Divine 2012)

There is a vast amount of resources available in regard to proper breathing techniques. Regardless of what type of lifestyle you are pursuing, you simply cannot afford to neglect addressing the area of proper breathing. It will allow you to be more patient in stressful situations, as well as provide much-needed rejuvenation, whether it be a peaceful night's sleep or taking a few minutes to quiet your mind while driving down the highway.

Cultivate Patience

The positive changes that you want to see in your life are not only possible, but achievable. But I urge you to remember that sometimes the most significant changes do not occur overnight. If you apply step 9 and not only learn but *cultivate patience*, you will begin to see all your dreams and desires come to fruition. In turn, you will finally be able to enjoy life and achieve the happiness that you've always dreamed of.

STEP 10

Never Stop Growing

"This is where your motivation is found."

Where to Now?

So now that we've laid the groundwork and provided insight on what it takes to create an amazing life, it is inevitable that some ask, "So the journey is complete, right? I've achieved happiness, and now I'm good to go."

The answer to this question is a profound no! This may lead one to then pose the question in an exasperated manner, "Does this mean that this process is never going to end?"

The answer is that the journey could stop here, but it shouldn't. At least it *should* never stop if you are sincere about moving toward, attaining, and maintaining a life full of fulfillment and happiness. Your reaction to this statement should not be one of trepidation, but rather one of excitement.

Far too often when we are journeying through life, we set goals and pursue endeavors, only to stop growing once those goals are achieved. This is a disastrous mistake that will inevitably lead you back to those dark places such as boredom, restlessness, and ultimate unhappiness.

Setting your sights on new goals to achieve and improvements to make pulls you forward in life and creates an environment of continual growth. If you reach a certain point in life and then decide to stop or stand still, then your life will become like stagnant water, impure and contaminated.

You see, happiness and fulfillment are not something to be achieved or a goal to be accomplished so that you can then just sit back, relax, and watch life pass you by. On the contrary, once you find the path and begin walking the path, it is imperative that you continue on the path. Continual growth is what creates excitement in your life and gives you a sense of purpose.

Despite the fact that you may have achieved a station in life that you are very pleased with and want to stay in that situation, it is important to realize that life never stands still.

As the Greek philosopher Heraclitus once said, "The only thing that is constant is change." Your life, even if it is going great, is going to change. But as we've discussed earlier, change should not infer change for the worse. On the contrary, it could and should mean change for the better.

It's Time to Write Your Next Chapter

Have you ever read a book you simply could not put down? Or perhaps you were so intrigued that you couldn't wait for a few minutes of free time to pick it up and read what happens next? The truth of the matter is that often times, our lives unfold like a real-life novel. We enjoy the early chapters of our life, including our childhood and high school. Most times after high school, we create a plan to establish a career, or possibly get married and start a family, but after that, far too often, the planning stops. College becomes a means to an end. For many, their only objective from then on becomes getting a secure job and hopefully finding an equilibrium until retirement.

Speaking from my own personal experience, once I had graduated college, the next objective was to find a secure job, establish a career, then sit back and enjoy life. I hadn't thought about what would give my life purpose and meaning beyond achieving that particular goal.

Throughout my experience, I have found that human beings have a tendency to seek a permanent solution or a cure-all in order to create a comfortable life. Most of us do what we need to do in order to fix a perceived problem and then go on with our lives in the same manner in which we always have.

If our car breaks down or the hot water heater stops working, we make a repair or call a professional to fix it so that life can go on. Most people adopt the philosophy of "if it's not broke, then don't fix it" for their lives.

But it's important to realize that our broken lives are not the same as an automobile or air conditioner that can simply be repaired and then will be good to go until we leave this earth.

You're An Artist

On the contrary, our lives should be seen as a work in progress or, even better, a work of *art* in progress. As the ten-time NCAA basketball championship winning Coach John Wooden once said, "Make each day your masterpiece."

Even if you've made substantial improvements to your life and are currently enjoying a great deal of happiness, it is essential to continually move forward and make a genuine effort to continue improving.

You see, the path isn't something to be found or discovered and then only used temporarily. The path is to be discovered and traveled upon for the rest of our earthly lives. As long as we are walking the path, we are living consciously, using all the tools and skills that we have developed along the way, continually growing and becoming more aware. As long as we walk the path, we can continue to grow and live happily according to God's will.

As we all know, life, as with time, never stops moving forward. It is up to you to determine which direction your life will go. If you stay aligned with the path of righteousness, there's a good chance that your life will turn out the way that you've always hoped that it would. On the other hand, if you stray from the path, you will simply find yourself lost again, disgruntled, unfulfilled, and unhappy.

This Is Great News!

We should all find great joy in this fact because what this means is that we get to continue improving, whether we're twenty, thirty, or even eighty years old and beyond. There has only been One to ever walk the earth that was perfect; therefore, we can always find areas in which we can focus our energy in order to improve.

To understand the essential reason for us to continue to evolve and progress further on the path, we need to look no further than many former professional athletes. In the world of professional sports, athletes retire at a relatively young age, which is considered completely normal in the competitive world, but not necessarily in the world outside of sports.

An Article published by Roosevelts.com in July of 2013, the average NFL career spans only 3.5 years and the average NBA career is only 4.8 years long.

Keep in mind that many of these athletes have been playing their respective sports for the majority of their lives before becoming a professional. And throughout those formative years, they have dedicated a significant portion of their lives to training in order to develop and improve upon their skills in their chosen sport.

After retirement, an athlete may realize that there is suddenly a huge void in their life. There is also an abundance of free time in their daily schedule that was formerly filled by the continual grind of moving on and up to the next level as, well as maintaining a full-time career.

After retirement, these athletes are still young by most standards and still have a considerable number of years left in their lives in which they can pursue other endeavors. Athletes must be extremely careful to maintain their desire and focus on pursuing other positive endeavors in which they can find meaning and fulfillment. Many retired athletes certainly do go on to become successful in other areas of life, but there are also those who get caught up in situations that are not so positive.

This is all compounded for many with a loss of identity after their competitive days are over. For many athletes, being an athlete becomes their identity; it's who they feel that they are. Therefore, once their playing days are over, their identity is lost. They're not quite sure who they are or what they should be doing with the rest of their lives.

Athletes become susceptible to things such as excessive partying and substance abuse in their desperate search for a high that can match the competitive field of play and offer them some way to continue feeling significant.

Many of us deal with similar feelings and challenges as some former professional athletes. We spend a number of years or a portion of our lives striving to attain certain goals or a particular station in life. Once we've reached our destination, we come to a standstill in our lives, uncertain as to where to go next.

If we do not promptly move forward to continue our progress and set new goals, we run the risk of allowing our lives to become stagnant and become susceptible to negativity in our lives.

A Price Must Be Paid

An important aspect to take note of in the pursuit of the life that you desire is that nothing that is worth achieving in life comes without a cost. There will always be a price to be paid. Just as our Lord and Savior sacrificed Himself so that we can attain eternal life, so too are you and I required to pay a price in order to achieve the life of our dreams.

Although our God loves us unconditionally and eternally, it is important to realize that He is fair and just as well. It would not be fair to just hand a happy life over to an individual through no effort of their own. But if we are willing to live a life that is pleasing to our Heavenly Father, then there is no limit as to what we may accomplish in this life.

Get Tough

If you are truly sincere about achieving a life of happiness and fulfillment, then it is absolutely essential that you are aware of and embrace one important notion. That notion is that at times in your life, you will have to get tough! Although this may seem like a somewhat vague statement, this is nonetheless one of the most vital components in creating the life of your dreams.

Allow me to elaborate. Although I do not doubt for a second your desire to achieve a happy life, there is no doubt that at some point, hardships and challenges will arise. After all, we all know that life has its ups and downs. When things do not seem to be going the way that you had planned in the pursuit of your goals, sometimes it just boils down to simply digging down deep and getting tough.

Dr. Angela Lee Duckworth of the University of Pennsylvania conducted an in-depth study into the mind-set of successful individuals in order to determine why some individuals accomplished their goals and followed through on what they had set out to do and why some fell short.

You see, Dr. Duckworth had been a teacher in the New York City school system, and what she had realized during her tenure as an educator was that although some students were much more gifted than others, those with greater talent were not always the ones to achieve the highest grades. This raised a number of questions in Dr. Duckworth's mind. She began to wonder what the key factor or factors were in determining the level of an individual's success.

Questions began to arise, such as, does talent play a role? Why is it that those who are naturally gifted or talented are not always the ones to succeed? Dr. Duckworth's team conducted studies at various locations in their quest to identify the determining factor of success, including the prestigious West Point Military Academy and even the National Spelling Bee. After a number of years of study, Dr. Duckworth concluded that the level of one's success boiled down to one important ingredient that cannot be quantitatively measured: grit (University of Pennsylvania Dr. Duckworth Research Statement).

Dr. Duckworth defined *grit* as "passion and perseverance for long-term goals." Although you cannot measure grit quantitatively, I agree with Dr. Duckworth's conclusion. I too have had the opportunity to work with individuals both as an educator and as a coach and will attest to the fact that oftentimes students and athletes who experience the most success were not nearly as naturally gifted as some of those in which they surpassed.

The bottom line is that more times than not, the difference between a person who is successful and a person who is not is not a matter of talent or ability, but rather a matter of desire. I absolutely agree with the conclusion of Dr. Duckworth, but rather than using the term *grit*, I've always simply referred to this key ingredient as plain old *toughness*.

There's a popular phrase among coaches that "hard work beats talent any day." Whether it was in the classroom or on the field of play, I've seen the truth in that very saying firsthand. I've had many students that were gifted intellectually struggling to get passing grades simply due to a lack of effort. Oftentimes it is referred to as being lazy. I would categorize it more as a lack of toughness.

On the other hand, I've experienced times when a student was not as gifted intellectually, but regardless of what they had lacked in natural ability, they studied, persevered, and did their homework, ultimately scoring one of the highest grades in the class. It was simply a matter of getting tough and putting in the work.

Got Heart? Try Wrestling

One of the things that always drew me to wrestling was the fact that it was a sport that rewarded hard work. Other sports oftentimes favor the person who is the fastest, the strongest, the biggest, or maybe even the tallest, basically, those who are more naturally gifted. But when it comes to wrestling, the most important quality that one can possess is heart.

The sport of wrestling utilizes weight classes. Therefore, it negates the advantage of one person being bigger and stronger than the other. In order to get a starting position in the lineup, an individual would have to win a "wrestle off" pitting one man against another. I always loved that aspect of the sport.

I was small in high school, and although I knew that I was tough and possessed a lot of heart, ultimately it was up to the coaches to decide who would start when it came to sports such as football. But in wrestling, whether or not you would be in the starting lineup was entirely up to you.

And for those who have never wrestled, I promise you that unless you've experienced it, you cannot imagine how exhausted you can get in six minutes. General Norman Schwarzkopf Jr., the leader of coalition forces in the first Persian Gulf War, once stated, "I would come out of football season and think that I was in pretty good shape and for about the first two weeks of wrestling season I'd throw up every single day because it was so grueling" (Dan Gable 2001).

As a coach, I was honored to coach a number of young men that, despite their lack of talent, were able to experience tremendous success on the wrestling mat through hard work.

One athlete in particular comes to mind when speaking of the value of hard work. He did not seem destined to enjoy any success whatsoever when he first came out for the team. During his freshman year, he was so out of shape that he could barely run a single lap around the track during conditioning and lost nearly every bout throughout both his freshman and sophomore seasons. I remember thinking to myself that this might be one of our athletes that will lose interest and quit the team.

But despite his lack of success, this young man continued to work hard and put in the time and effort necessary to improve. Sure enough, this athlete's hard work began to pay off. As a matter of fact, he not only made the varsity lineup, he went on to qualify for the state championships during his senior season.

It was extremely rewarding to see this young man surpass all expectations during his career. Not only was the entire coaching staff proud of his accomplishments, but the sense of accomplishment and newfound confidence that this young man had achieved through his efforts were evident upon his face when he punched his ticket to the championships.

So what does all this have to do with your life? The point that I'm trying to get across is that whether it be in the classroom, on the wrestling mat, or in the business world, the person who accomplishes what they set out to do in life is the one who is willing to get tough and overcome all obstacles in their path.

Most likely, in your pursuit of happiness, there will come a time when you begin to question whether or not it's all worth it. You may ask yourself, "Is this sacrifice really worth the effort?" You may even tell yourself that things aren't so bad the way that they are. If you find yourself saying these types of things, snap out of it! Get tough and keep moving forward. And remember that the life that you deserve is waiting.

The Secret to Success: Hard Work

Oftentimes coaches throughout the country and even the world would seek to discover Dan Gable's secret to overwhelming success in wrestling, both as an athlete and especially as a coach. How was it that this man was able to coach his team to an amazing record of 355–21–5 (dangable.com)?

According to Dan Gable himself, the secret is that there is no secret. Gable's athletes will attest to this fact. It was no surprise to them that they were able to win an amazing fifteen NCAA national team titles under Gable's tutelage. The reason that it was no surprise was that they were part of a program that established and valued hard work as the cornerstone to their success.

As a matter of fact, Coach Gable's workouts were so notoriously hard that two-time NCAA wrestling champion Royce Alger would use the word *torture* to describe the Iowa practices, and even went on to say, "I'd rather do time than go back and do some of that stuff" (Dan Gable 2001).

Dan Gable did not try to hide or keep this a secret from the rest of the world. As a matter of fact, Gable was very open and honest when speaking of his method of success. Gable once said, "Human nature is to find an easy way of doing things" (*Dan Gable: Competitor Supreme* 1991). This is evident in virtually every aspect of society in which we see technology and machines that make our lives easier.

But what Gable was trying to convey is that sometimes you simply cannot replace the value of hard work. Sometimes there is no other way to achieve a goal than to put your nose to the grindstone and work hard.

The same can also be said for creating the life of your dreams. Whether you are striving to purchase your dream home or mend the damages of a broken marriage, the fact of the matter is that you will at times need to put aside the excuses and just plain work hard. The ability of working hard is simply a matter of mindset. Mental toughness and fortitude are developed by pushing oneself a little further each day while stating focused on your goals. When you find yourself struggling to stay motivated, ask yourself one simple question, "How bad do I want this?" The answer should be easy.

Sweet Success

On your journey to creating an amazing life, you may find yourself asking, "Why does this have to be so hard? Why couldn't I have just inherited the life of my dreams?" These are fair questions, and I understand why one may ask them. The reality is that you should see the opportunity to work hard to create an amazing life as a blessing. The truth is that when we put forth a great effort in order to achieve something, it makes the achievement that much more gratifying. I wrote the following equation in regard to work and its relationship to a sense of accomplishment.

I've seen some of the toughest men and women in the world sobbing at the top of the podium at the Olympic Games after winning the gold medal. Some may wonder why an individual of such great strength would feel so overwhelmed with emotion. The fact of the matter is that an accomplishment so great must be pursued and worked toward for years. These individuals have sacrificed immense amounts of time, leisure, relationships, not to mention a tremendous amount of blood, sweat, and tears, some since grade school, in order to accomplish this feat. Oftentimes the sense of accomplishment can be so great that the emotions associated can become overwhelming.

The fact of the matter is that no matter what the endeavor, whether it be pursuing your black belt in jujitsu or getting your master's degree, you can find motivation in knowing that the amount of effort put forth will be directly proportional to the sense of accomplishment that you will feel after you have accomplished that goal.

Your Father in heaven wants you to realize and appreciate the value of the achievements that you are going to accomplish in life. Just as any endeavor that you may pursue in life, if you attain it easily, it will not carry as much meaning. National champion NCAA wrestling coach and Vietnam veteran J. Robinson once stated that "the more that you have invested in something, the harder it is to let go" (*Keepers of the Flame*, Flowrestling.org, 2016).

Therefore, stay in faith and in a positive mind-set when pursuing your goals because when you achieve them, it will be that much more rewarding!

Strive for Perfection

There is no doubt that we all have our faults. As mentioned earlier, there has only been One to have walked the earth perfect and sinless. But understanding that we are flawed should not serve as an excuse to lower the standard by which we live. No one on earth is perfect, but just because perfection is unattainable doesn't mean that we shouldn't strive to achieve it. It was none other than Jesus Himself Who said, "Be perfect, as your Father in Heaven is perfect." (Matthew 5:48)

Therefore, it is of vital importance that you should continue moving forward on the path and continue to live a life of meaning and purpose. If you continue to do so, upon reaching the twilight of your years, you can look back with a great sense of fulfillment and gratitude for the tremendous quality of life that you were able to experience throughout the years.

It pleases God when we strive to be the best that we can possibly be. We are all blessed with a certain amount of potential in various areas. And although no one will ever completely fulfill their potential, we still need to do our very best to try.

I believe that there are few greater tragedies in life than when an individual fulfills virtually none of their God-given potential. As a teacher and coach, it was always such a tremendous disappointment to see great talent and ability go to waste.

I sometimes wonder if the brilliant mind that was destined to cure cancer was squandered, consumed by meaningless endeavors such as video games. Or perhaps the individual that is meant to discover the ability to travel at the speed of light will be too distracted by television or social media to even get off the couch. What a tragedy this would be. Pursuing goals and continuing to grow fills your life with enthusiasm and purpose. I urge you, do not allow the potential with which you have been blessed go to waste. Do your best to fulfill your potential and reach your destiny.

It's Not Over

I implore you, do not make the mistake that is oftentimes made by so many others. So many times, after a tremendous amount of progress is made, individuals think that their journey is over. They stop moving forward. Please do not allow this journey of personal growth to end here. Continue to utilize this book. Refresh your memory when it is needed. Refer to passages time and again. Share this book with a friend. Help others to achieve happiness as well. And most of all, never stop growing!

It's time to get excited about life. Your journey should not end here. As a matter of fact, you should be excited that you can and should continue to grow until your days on earth are over. By implementing step 10 and reminding yourself that you will *never stop growing*, you will undoubtedly attain the fulfillment and happiness that you've always desired.

Conclusion

Happiness Awaits

As mentioned at the beginning of this book, I truly believe that life is meant to be enjoyed. I also believe that our Heavenly Father wants nothing more than for you, me, and everyone in the world for that matter to be happy. Unfortunately, I believe that only a few will actually ever achieve a life of happiness.

I have shown you the path, but it is up to you whether or not you will walk it. You have the power to live the life that you've always dreamed of. Now the rest is up to you.

Therefore, I implore you, take advantage of God's blessings. Make the most out of this life. God always offers us a choice. He would never force us to do anything against our will. It is up to you to take the necessary steps. Don't waste another minute of this precious life unhappy and empty, chasing meaningless pursuits. Live the life that you've always dreamed of. Find meaning and purpose. Live a life that is full and happy. Live a life that you, as well as others, can respect and admire. Walk the path that will please your Heavenly Father, as well as bring joy, fulfillment, and happiness to you and your loved ones. Don't look back for a second. There is absolutely no reason that the amazing life that God has in store for you cannot become your reality.

I firmly believe that if you follow the steps that have been laid out before you, there is no limit on what you can accomplish! Good luck and God bless!

Sources

1. Blaszczak-Boxe.Agata, "Americans more depressed now than decades ago." October 2, 2014. http://www.cbsnews.com/news/americans more-depressed-now-than-decades-ago/

2. Divine.Mark. "The Big Four of Mental Toughness: Part 2." April 19, 2012. http://sealfit.com/the-big-4-of-mental-toughness-part-2/

3. Duckworth, Angela L. August 9, 2012 https://www.sas.upenn.edu/~duckwort/images/current/researchstatement080912.pdf

4. Frankl.Viktor. Man's Search for Meaning

5. Gladwell.Malcolm. Blink

6. Holcombe.Kate. "Breathe Easy with Pranayama." June 15, 2012. http://www.yogajournal.com/article/practice-section/healing-breath/

7. Nelson.Jeff, "The Longest Professional Sports Careers." July 22, 2013. http://www.rsvlts.com/2013/07/22/longest-sports-careers/

8. Ridley.Matt. The Rational Optimist

9. Ross.Hugh, "Probability for Life on Earth." April 1, 2004 www.reasons.org/articles/probability-for-life-on-earth.

10. Wolf-Mann. Ethan "The Average American is in Credit Card Debt No Matter the Economy." February 9, 2016. http://time.com/money/4213757/average-american-credit-card-debt/

11. Woodall.Candy, "Prayers help Lancaster's Nickel Mines heal years after Amish school shooting." October 2, 2015. http://www.pennlive.com.

12. Worstall.Tim, "Astonishing Numbers: America's Poor Still Lives Better Than Most of Humanity" June 1, 2003. http://www.forbes.com/sites/timworstall/2013/06/01/astonishing-numbers-americas-poor-still-live-better-than-most-of-the-rest-of-humanity/#5e443a6823c4

13. A Football Life. "Dick Vermeil." NFL Network. October 30, 2015

14. Keepers of the Flame. Flowresting.org. February 10, 2016.

15. Dan Gable: Competitor Supreme. Giant Step Productions, 1992. VHS

16. ESPN SportsCentury. "Dan Gable." ESPN. April 27, 2001.

17. Teddy Roosevelt: An American Lion. Directed by David de Vries. USA: A and E Home Video, 2003. DVD

18. http://www.timeanddate.com/time/international-atomic-time.html.

19. http://www.stress.org/stress-is-killing-you/

20. http://www.Dangable.com/bio/

21. http://www.theheartfoundation.org/heart-disease-facts/heart-disease-statistics/

22. http://www.webmd

23. http://www.aans.org/Patient%20Information/Conditions%20and%20Treatments/Low%20Back%20Pain.aspx

24. http://www.npr.org/templates/story/story.php?storyId=90638364

ABOUT THE AUTHOR

William Russell English is a former wrestler, championship coach, Air Force veteran, author, philosopher, and teacher. He has gained invaluable experience through years of wrestling training and coaching, time spent in the military, and his tenure as a teacher. He has spent over a decade developing a philosophy and system on how to attain happiness and fulfillment. He lives with his wife Stephanie in Pennsylvania.

CPSIA information can be obtained
at www.ICGtesting.com
Printed in the USA
FSOW01n0813310317
32561FS